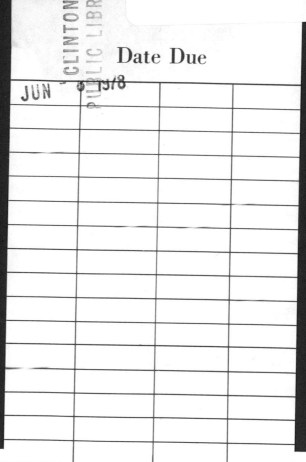

338
.0924
Freim

Freiman, Lawrence, 1909–
    Don't fall off the rocking horse; an
autobiography. Toronto, McClelland
and Stewart, 1978.
    199 p. illus

1. Freiman, Lawrence, 1909–
2. Businessmen – Canada – Biography.
I. Title.
0771031815   0511889

6/el/en

DON'T FALL OFF THE ROCKING HORSE

DON'T FALL OFF THE ROCKING HORSE

An Autobiography

Lawrence Freiman

McCLELLAND AND STEWART

For Audrey,
Our Children,
And Theirs.

CANADIAN CATALOGUING IN PUBLICATION DATA

Freiman, Lawrence, 1909-
  Don't fall off the rocking horse

ISBN 0-7710-3181-5

1. Freiman, Lawrence, 1909-   2. Businessmen
- Canada - Biography. I. Title.

HC112.5.F74A3   338'.092'4   C77-001815-7

Printed and Bound in Canada

Table of Contents

Acknowledgements

Many people have been helpful to me in writing this book. I am grateful to the late Lyla Rasminsky for telling me to write a book, for buying the pens, paper, and dictionary, and directing me to "get on with it." Bernard Figler's biography of my parents, *Lillian and Archie Freiman*, has been of great help, and with his permission I have utilized significant information. I would like to take this opportunity to say how pleased I am with his work.

In addition, I would like to thank the following people: Dr. June Forsyth for working with me in editing the first draft of the manuscript; Klaus Jochem for certain detailed research; R.E.G. Davis, formerly Executive Director of the Canadian Welfare Council, for his research relating to the council; Ross McLean, formerly Acting Commissioner of the National Film Board of Canada; and Mary Kosalle, formerly fashion co-ordinator for Freiman's, for information they provided; and Garth Hopkins for editing the manuscript. For their assistance I also want to thank my friends Tom Patterson, David Haber, Bill Boss, Peter Kriendler, and Maxwell Meighen. Finally, I am grateful to the late Grace Nadeau, my former secretary, for her patience in deciphering the many handwritten pages and for typing the manuscript.

Foreword

It is pompous to write an autobiography, suggests Pablo Casals. He settles for *Reflections of Casals*. I not only agree with him, but I believe that autobiographies should not be reserved for certain categories of ladies and gentlemen who persist in writing them. Included in these categories are retired generals years after the battles they engaged in are over; ex-heads of state; former dedicated secretaries of Prime Ministers and diplomats, their elderly former lovers, or their butlers on small pensions who might have voyeuristic, maudlin secrets to market. Another category of these writers is artists. Their lives should be recalled by daughters who are, although voluble, extremely tender. There is also the actor category, probably the most egotistically boring of all.* Actors usually write with great ebullience, lacking any inhibition whatsoever. Inevitably, these ladies and gentlemen turn up on television talk shows and, with some reservations, thrust their books forward so the camera can pan in and carry an enlarged image to an unsuspecting public composed mainly of elderly housewives and teenage girls, referred to by networks as "the afternoon viewing public." Finally, not the least important of the memoir writers, is the courtesan. She stretches from biblical times to Dubarry, to Xaviera Hollander and her wistfully titled *The Happy Hooker*.

With all my reservations I still feel compelled to glimpse into the delicate autobiographical area. I do not see myself as mighty or meek, particularly sinful or witty—yet I want to look homeward at the variety of people who have "touched" me. Unlike Thomas Wolfe, I can go home again because I never left the place where there were and are happy times—Ottawa. I want to look to time past, and to people who are special to me, hoping that some of them might become special to others. My good fortune of time and place is to have been part of a simple, gentle, and graceful earlier time when we were more innocent. My hope is to share a view of the present by looking through both ends of my own time's telescope.

*Please exclude David Niven's charming *The Moon is a Balloon*.

7

Some of my contemporaries may be critical of certain information they may wish to fault as not being factual. They might be right. Memory tends to be capricious and part fantasy. For my part, it matters only that the reflections are as I remember them. They are my impressions, hopefully enlarged as they are shared. My kaleidoscope turns in changing patterns from the house of my grandfather to those of my mother, my father, and my own. I see my father's Cadillac Four when I was very young, and the red Stutz I had at McGill University. I see the Parliament Buildings against the lush greens, reds, and yellows of leaves turning colour in the thousands of acres of Gatineau Park. I also see stages at Stratford and Tom Patterson and Tyrone Guthrie there. I see the 1969 opening of the National Arts Centre and a vista of orange groves in Israel. My kaleidoscope turns from Jan Peerce in the Russian Tea Room in New York to David Ben-Gurion and Moshe Sharett in Israel, from Regina Resnick to Golda Meir, from the late afternoons and evenings with Peter Kriendler and the boys at 21 to a careful upside, downside look at the decorative, bounteous Gabors and the other richly endowed ladies who adorn Charlie Farrel's Racquet Club at Palm Springs. The settings change from the Savoy in London to the Excelsior in Rome and the King David in Jerusalem. Included is the small rocking horse that I played on as a child in my room. It bobbed up and down slowly with a gentle rhythm. It was difficult, if not impossible, to fall off. Time, however, brings its own mutation. The variations and changes become greater. The "ups" become always higher and more difficult to achieve. The "lows" become steeper and more dangerous. The fortunate hear the timeless voices of those who have "touched" them at unknown moments or in the quiet of the night—the voice that warns "don't fall off." Through all of these images stands our store—Freiman's—in its singularly strange, perhaps too compelling relationship to my life.

As I dwelt in the houses of my grandfather, my mother, my father, and my own with my wife and children, I have dwelt in Israel, the eternal house of our people. Each furnished its own fullness—and provided a doorway opening into the adjoining one. Something will remain. I have yet to approach the next house.

8

Chapter I

My Grandfather's House

The night of June 2, 1969, was an unlikely moment to remember Moses Bilsky–my grandfather, and Ottawa's first Jew.

It was a warm, fragrant night, filled with pomp and glitter. Hamilton Southam and I, playing our respective white tie, be-medalled roles of Director General and Chairman of the National Arts Centre, had just welcomed their Excellencies the Governor General and Mrs. Michener to the centre's gala opening ceremonies.

Standing there in the foyer of the incredibly beautiful opera house, it suddenly occurred to me what a short moment it had been since those same grounds on Confederation Square had echoed with the raucous, drunken brawls of Irish and French Canadian lumberjacks.

Those were the mid-nineteenth-century days, when Ottawa was one of the roughest, toughest towns in North America–the days when Moses Bilsky sold great gold Beau Brummel like watches and fobs to the burly, boisterous men who crowded into his little shop just east of what was later to be Ottawa's Union

Station. The lumbermen were paid every Saturday evening: $4 for a ten-hour day, six days a week. Saturday night, from the camps of the lumber barons – MacKay, Bronson, Gilmour, Fauquier, Booth, and Eddy, whose sprawling mills clustered around Chaudière Falls on the Ottawa River below the present Parliament buildings – the men would stream into town to drink and fight and love, and often to buy great gold watches and fobs from Moses Bilsky.

From this beginning, Grandfather soon built his business to the point where he could open a fine jewellery store in what is now Confederation Square. That was the start of his comfortable years in Ottawa; comfortable, that is, for the times and compared to his younger days of far-flung adventure.

Moses Bilsky arrived in Ottawa in 1857, ten years before Confederation and a little more than one hundred years before the opening of the National Arts Centre. He was twenty-eight years old and filled with the spirit of adventure. He had come to Canada with his father, Ely, in 1845, after spending two years in New York, where his father had emigrated from Lithuania. The Bilskys went first to Montreal and later to Kemptville, a thriving lumber town, twenty-five miles south of "Bytown," where the youthful Moses often visited, sometimes on business for his merchant father. In 1857, Ely Bilsky sold his business and left for Palestine to wait out his years, as was the custom then among religious Jews. Moses, with nothing to keep him in Kemptville, decided to live in Ottawa, which "Bytown" had been named when it was incorporated as a city in 1854. His arrival marked the beginning of a life-long love affair with the city that, despite numerous absences from it, was always home.

Tall and broad of physique, vigorous in speech and action, and brimming with restless energy, Grandfather found the frontier life of Ottawa very much to his liking. But in time, new frontiers called. In 1861, lured by heady tales of the gold rush, he trekked to British Columbia's remote Caribou country where, like so many others, he found only cold and hard work. In later years he would say of the gold rush: "Prices were too goddamn high out there. If you didn't find gold it was impossible to buy anything. Everything was so expensive." To finance his return east, Grandfather had to hire himself out carrying nails up the

10

side of a mountain where sluices were being built to separate gold from gravel; horses and mules, it seems, were practically non-existent and very expensive, and strong young men were at a premium.

So Moses Bilsky returned to Ottawa, only to be lured away again, this time by the excitement of the American Civil War. He headed south and joined the Union Army, moving with his unit across the Isthmus of Panama to California, where the soldiers were used to suppress the riots that flared in San Francisco after President Lincoln was assassinated at the Ford Theatre in Washington on April 14, 1865. After the war, Ottawa's "wandering Jew," it has been written,* unsuspectingly found himself working as a gun-runner for the highest bidder in the Mexican-Maximillian encounter. He had been chosen for his size and strength from a crowd of volunteers to perform an unspecified task. He was shocked to learn after a time what he was doing, so he quit and returned once again to Ottawa.

I heard these and other stories many years later in my grandfather's fine Victorian house on Nicholas Street. I often went there for lunch after Sabbath services in the synagogue. After lunch there was always "one more story."

He told about the time in his life when he decided that his wanderings were over. It was time to settle down. He was forty-five in 1874 when he met my grandmother, Pauline Reich, in Brooklyn. She was sixteen. At that point in his life, Grandfather had amassed a wealth of experience, and very little else—a serious obstacle for a would-be suitor. Undeterred, he asked Pauline's father for permission to marry her, indicating that the lumber mill he owned in Montreal made him a man of considerable substance. His intended father-in-law said he would be pleased to visit Grandfather and take a look at the mill.

Fortunately, Grandfather had a friend in Montreal who did indeed own a mill, and he hastened back to Canada to prepare for Mr. Reich's visit. It was duly arranged that when Mr. Reich arrived, his future son-in-law would be ensconced behind his friend's massive roll-top desk to receive his guest. The foreman would then be called to take the visitor on a tour of the mill,

*In Figler, Bernard, *Lillian and Archie Freiman* (Montreal: 1962).

11

since Grandfather knew nothing of the mill's operation. The plan worked without a hitch, and Mr. Reich was properly impressed with Grandfather and his financial situation. The marriage accordingly took place in Brooklyn in 1874.

Years later Grandfather told me how, at one point, they moved to Ottawa and then to a small cabin in the boisterous lumber town of Mattawa, about 150 miles northwest of Ottawa, where life must have been very hard indeed for the youthful Mrs. Bilsky. After a time they moved to Montreal and then back to Ottawa. Moses Bilsky was "home" again, and my grandmother never told her parents the story of their first difficult years until long after Grandfather had established his fine jewellery business and their comfortable way of life in Ottawa.

In that lively Jewish household there were eventually eleven children of their own, plus twin nieces who came to stay after their mother, Grandfather's sister, died. Adding to the already large household was a steady stream of visiting friends and other guests. I can still remember the wonderful dark, carved mahogany furniture with antimacassars in the drawing room, and the large verandah that overlooked the garden facing the Rideau Canal. Father told us, recalling his days of courting Mother, that Saturday night in this large house was poker night, a long, rather raucous affair with great mounds of sandwiches, large cuts of roast beef, and quantities of beer and more substantial drink. Grandfather presided over this scene, joined by his older sons and the better Irish poker players of the neighbourhood.

This area was the centre of Ottawa's Irish population at that time, and it was no accident that the University of Ottawa was then predominantly Irish Catholic. Nor was it any accident that from here developed the famous Silver Seven hockey team, and the lacrosse and hockey teams of the Shamrock Athletic Club, of which, I have been told, one of my uncles, Sam Bilsky, one of Ottawa's most noted sportsmen, served for a time as President.

These teams brought great lustre to the city, for they boasted such hockey greats as Harvey Pulford, the great all-round athlete of his time, the Gilmour brothers, Frank McGee, and Harry Westwick. Bill Westwick, his son, was in the same year as I in high school, and he went on to become one of the country's foremost sportswriters. He recalled to me a short time ago (and I

12

remember so well) the window in my grandfather's jewellery store that displayed the gold pocket watches that would be presented to each member of the Ottawa Senators. They had just won the NHL championship by defeating Vancouver and were to return to Ottawa the next day.

The world of my grandfather really began for me with his next home on Daly Avenue. It was there that I so frequently spent the Sabbath evenings and from there that he lit the long, twisted candle and recited the Havdalah prayer at sundown and sipped wine, shared with the family, to mark the end of the Sabbath day.

The synagogue played a dominant role in Grandfather's life. He told me that it took several years before there was a Minyan, which requires ten Jews over thirteen years of age for a religious service. When the tenth arrived in Ottawa, and some of Grandfather's sons were over thirteen, religious services were held in Grandfather's house. After the visitors arrived and had tethered their horses, the Friday-night service began. They would spend the night, and services began again on the Sabbath morning.

Although Grandfather was actively involved in Ottawa's growing Jewish community, neither he nor his colleagues ever thought that they were planning or structuring a framework for the future. In those early days, if it was necessary to have ten Jews to hold a formal service, it was done not with the idea of beginning a synagogue but because it was an injunction of the Lord to have ten Jews in attendance at a service. When more Jews came into the community a larger place was needed for worship, so a larger place was acquired. It was a simple response to a religious requirement that, with the help of Grandfather, established the Adath Jeshurum congregation and produced Ottawa's first synagogue on Murray Street in 1892. A different kind of necessity produced the second. Not long after it opened, the congregation discovered that the prevailing winds in the area carried various aromas from a food processing plant nearby. Highly noticeable among these aromas was the smell of cooking pork, which quite often swirled through the synagogue during Sabbath service. This undesirable situation led to the development of a larger synagogue on King Edward Avenue. It was to this synagogue that I went every Sabbath with my grandfather. What seemed so large then is now a small memorial chapel.

It was deemed necessary that the new synagogue have a reverend gentleman of religious authority to act as cantor and to supervise Jewish ceremonies. Grandfather was entrusted with the assignment of going to New York to choose the right man. He did so, and after the choice had been made, Grandfather purchased the first scrolls of the Torah. The two men then set out for Ottawa by train, taking turns sleeping so that one could hold the Torah upright, making certain that it would not fall. The custom was that such a calamity was a bad omen that could be offset only by a twenty-four hour fast.

The synagogue brought great happiness to Grandfather, and each Sabbath was a very holy day, a day to be sanctified. Because I was so frequently included in his Sabbath days, they were also days of great happiness for me. After synagogue, we would return to the great house to partake of the vast luncheon feast that Grandfather so enjoyed; as an Orthodox Jew, he would not eat breakfast before attending synagogue. His orthodoxy gave him much joy, as for grandfather Jewish law was simple. You either followed it completely or you were guilty of religious misdemeanours. This was not to say that one could not negotiate certain "arrangements" with the Lord, and Grandfather did. He was, for example, an avid boxing fan. But the fights were held on Friday nights in the Drill Hall; clearly, an "arrangement" had to be negotiated. Grandfather, after careful thought, concluded that if one of his sons purchased the tickets to the fight before the Sabbath, and if Grandfather went to the synagogue, and then walked from his home to the fight in rain, cold, snow, or sleet, the Lord would find this satisfactory. The tickets had not been purchased on the Sabbath, he had attended the synagogue, and he had walked, not ridden, to the Drill Hall. From his point of view, and certainly from mine when he took me, it was a splendid arrangement.

For all his orthodoxy and religious conviction, Grandfather had a salty streak that was frequently given voice. He was approached one day by Thomas Ahearn, who was proposing to organize the Ottawa Electric Railway to bring streetcar service to the growing city.

"Bilsky," his caller began, "I'm going to build a streetcar line. We're going to have horseless carriages run by electricity."

14

Grandfather snorted. "Of all the silly goddamn ideas I have ever heard. I don't believe coaches can run without horses. Never! That's impossible!" Right or wrong, Grandfather never hesitated to say what he thought.

It was that simple directness of approach to all things that made Grandfather the revered and respected man he always was in Ottawa. An active Zionist, he reported to the Zionist Federation in 1899 that a Zionist Society had been formed in Ottawa. Less than a year later, he was able to inform the First Zionist Convention that the Ottawa Society now had fifty members. In Zionist work, as in all things, his wife Pauline was at his side; she was a leading spirit in the formation of a Ladies' Auxiliary and was later named its Honorary President.

I remember being asked some years ago if Moses Bilsky, as the first Jew in Ottawa, had felt a sense of isolation or had faced prejudice and persecution. The question surprised me, and I waited several moments before replying, thinking quickly back over the many conversations I had had with Grandfather. "No, none," I replied. "I doubt that he ever thought about the possibility of such a thing. He was too honest, too gregarious, and so natural and forthright about life and his role in it that I simply can't imagine anyone not accepting him as the man he was."

Moses Bilsky retired from business when he was in his early sixties, and spent the next thirty years doing the things he liked. One of the things he liked best was to play checkers, and one of his favourite opponents was Mr. Dawson, governor of the Ottawa "gaol." All through my boyhood this spelling over the jail entrance, directly above where the two men battled over the checkerboard, always amazed and puzzled me.

Years later, after I returned to Ottawa from university, Mr. Dawson saw me one day and asked if I was Moses Bilsky's grandson. When I assured him that I was, he beamed and told me a story about Grandfather that I cherish still. Just before one of the Jewish High Holy Days many years before, Grandfather had heard that a Jew was being held in the jail. He strode up to the jail door, crackling with bad temper, and demanded that Governor Dawson give him the keys to the prisoner's cell. The governor inquired mildly as to why he should do that, and was told bluntly that no Jew should be in jail over the High Holy Days.

The governor silently handed the keys to Grandfather, who unlocked the cell and took the prisoner to his home, on the understanding that he would be returned after the High Holy Days. In due course Grandfather reappeared at the jail with his charge in tow. "Now that the High Holy Days are over, you can have the sonofabitch," he proclaimed. "No Jew should have been in jail in the first place, but certainly not during High Holy Days." With that, he spun on his heels and marched out.

Chief of Police Joliette, father of the famed hockey player Aurèle Joliette of the Montreal Canadiens, also told me sometime later that whenever he saw my grandfather approaching, he would immediately summon an officer to see if there was a Jewish person being held. He knew that Grandfather would try to get him released, irrespective of innocence or guilt.

Another pastime that Grandfather enjoyed enormously was spending summer afternoons riding behind the railing at the rear of the streetcars – those same horseless carriages he had so loudly denounced as impossible – talking to the conductors. I saw him many times, just riding and talking and looking. I think those streetcars intrigued him more than most of the many wonders he had seen in his long lifetime.

But there were more serious aspects to life at that time, too. After the pogroms in Russia and Poland, many Jews came to the United States and Canada. A number found their way to Ottawa; they could not speak English, they had no food, no shelter, and very few belongings. Their needs became Grandfather's first priority. After he found lodgings for a family, he took it upon himself to "look after" them, and he was seen on many a Sabbath evening pulling a sled through the snow with food and clothing and blankets all tied together with a rope, so that a newly arrived family could survive the first critical nights. Then, during the days, he went about the difficult task of finding jobs for them.

Moses Bilsky was a genial, generous, blasphemous, and thoroughly orthodox Jew – the patriarch of his community.

In 1922, the year before he died, a still vigorous ninety-three-year-old, he attended my Bar Mitzvah. On that day, I felt part of his great spirit pass to me, marking the continuation of my grandfather's house.

Chapter II

I Remember a Big House...and a BIGGER HOUSE

Life for me began in the large, red brick house on Russell Avenue, where Mother and Father settled soon after their marriage in 1903.

I am sure that my arrival in the winter of 1909 did little to disturb the serenity of those times. Sister Dorothy had preceded me by nearly three years, and in those days the second-born was an event of no great import.

My first memories are of size. The house was big, my parents were big, the street was big. Everything and everybody in the world was big—except Dorothy, who was just bigger than I was.

When I was four, we moved to the house on Somerset Street, and the scale of size took yet another leap. Three drawing rooms, the jungle-like conservatory with seemingly millions of tropical and other plants, the billiard room off the large library downstairs—all marvellously vast places for a boy to run, to hide, and to play. I remember every piece of furniture, the feel of the fabrics, the green tapestry border around the formal dining room at the top of the mahogany-panelled walls. It was a thoroughly magical house, and the many memories of childhood there warm me still.

The house had been built by C.P. Pattee in the late 1800-days of the lumber barons, and no detail had been spared. The mahogany room alone took six months to complete. There, Persian carpets littered the floor, with its foot-square sections of oak parquet–stepping stones to the leaded-glass bay windows with their cushioned window-seats where one could sit and dream and watch the world. I especially remember the magnificent bear skins, one brown and one white, that dominated one end of the room. When the adults gathered for after-dinner talk, I would hide under the skins, half suffocated by their heavy, blue felt lining and totally confident that because everyone pretended not to see me I was indeed invisible, even when scrambling beneath them on hands and knees.

On the second floor were Mother and Dad's massive bedroom and adjoining bath and the large guest room with its colossal bathroom. The third floor housed my bedroom, three others for the girls and guests, and two bathrooms.

My younger sister Queene was born some years after we moved to the house on Somerset. Her given name was Queen Esther, sparked no doubt by a burst of historical fervour in my parents. Whatever the reason, the name was heartily disliked by the other children, and soon became simply Queene, a thoroughly appropriate name for the lady of taste, distinction, and elegance that she became. Some years later in 1921, Gladys, a twelve-year-old war orphan, also came to the family, and the third floor was filled.

Seven of the eight servants–housekeeper, laundress, cook and her assistant, two upstairs maids, and the butler–lived in tiny quarters on the second floor, sharing one bathroom. The chauffeur did not live in.

The early memory montage also includes the Model School on Cartier Street, three blocks from home. Kindergarten there was a new world, a world of children, of games, of paper-cutting and modelling clay, and of noisy anarchy of the kind that only

18

healthy, high-spirited children can create. Our teacher, Miss Klotz, was a large woman, her heavy, white hair crowned always with a circular braid. Whether she was simply kind enough to permit our anarchy or powerless to stop it, I don't recall. But Jack Charleston, Graham Mayberry, Tom Carson, Tom Fuller, Phillip Foran, at least one Thorburn, and I, made for an imaginative, if less than serene, social unit.

Then came wonderful things like a punching bag for my room, games to play, metal soldiers, wonderful candles – and the times Mother would take us to Page and Shaw's ice cream parlour on the north side of Sparks Street between Elgin and Metcalfe. There we watched the ceiling fans slowly revolving as we sat in mahogany chairs with wicker seats and pink chintz covers and ate that gorgeous ice cream.

During those early days, the city of Ottawa was as magical as the house on Somerset. I knew that certain of the "big" people were somehow different, such as the man who lived around the corner from Russell Avenue on Chapel and Laurier, the street named after him. I can just remember seeing him in the splendour of his Prince Albert suit with the silk lapels and grey ascot and large pearl pin that looked frozen in the perfect folds of the ascot. When he said good day to my mother as he took his daily constitutional, his silk hat was swept high in a great arc, and his bow was low. Everything he did bespoke grace and distinction. Looking back, I am sure there must have been a great "Lauriermania." It was not a "swinging" time, in today's terms, but women must have tingled at his good looks, his charm, and his intellect. Had there been political polls, on radio and television, as we know them today, Sir Wilfred Laurier might have won the election of 1911, "Reciprocity and the Americans" notwithstanding.

However the women may have reacted to the elegant Prime Minister, sister Dorothy was not awed in his presence. One day, Mother, with Dorothy in tow, decided to return from downtown by streetcar. Dorothy, even at that early age, resented streetcars and the *hoi polloi*. She particularly resented the fact that our great new car had not been called. Among those seated in the streetcar was the gracious Sir Wilfred, who rose and offered Mother his seat. That did it for Dorothy. If she had to ride this dreadful machine, she had to do it seated or her dignity would be forever shattered. She protested loudly, and humiliation engulfed Mother. A vigorous pinch on Dorothy's leg was a stern signal to be quiet. The strategy failed, and Dorothy's further protests rang through the streetcar. Later, at home, Father was summoned from the store. His frosty countenance and reprimands cowed her into silence.

Dorothy's disappointment at not being able to ride in the family car was quite understandable and thoroughly consistent with my youthful logic. The car was unquestionably the greatest thing that had happened in my life to that point and of course anyone would prefer it to the streetcar. It had a shiny brass radiator, beautiful black shellacked running-boards, huge side lights, and fenders that turned up at the back. It was an immense thing, with a sliding glass partition separating front and back seats. A cut-glass vase, secure in a metal ring just behind the glass partition on the right-hand side, held a pink artificial rose. The back seat was covered with deep blue upholstery and two jump seats were protected with white and pink flowered slipcovers. The front seat was done in soft black leather and could accommodate two-and-a-half people. I was usually the one half. But the most wondrous part of all about the car was the "other" body. Come spring, the limousine body was simply lifted off the chassis. Aided by a few mysterious mechanical wonders, and enough men to do the lifting, the rather staid limousine was transformed into a nifty touring-car. On fine Sundays in spring and early summer, the touring-car top could be put down and we would set off, Mother and Father looking very snappy in their dusters and caps and goggles. These were intrepid journeys.

A drive to Britannia and back through sand and potholes took an afternoon and early evening. Once home, there was supper, one last look at the garden, and deep, tranquil sleep. In retrospect, Britannia was a combination of Coney Island, Capri, and the Lido, all wrapped into one exciting entertainment package. A great wooden walkway bisected the beach. On one side stood the Pavilion. On the other was a children's gourmet paradise abounding with ice cream cones, crackerjacks and indescribable delicacies. And there was the merry-go-round, with its large brown and white wooden horses astride shiny brass poles, bobbing up and down to loud hurdy-gurdy organ-grinder music.

There were other wonders at Britannia. One was the long, wooden pier over the water out to the Clubhouse, where the *G.B. Greene*, a great paddle-boat that took adults for day cruises on Lake Deschenes, was berthed. Another wonder was the auditorium. In later years, when we had our cottage nearby, I was permitted to go to the Saturday afternoon movies to see Pearl White serials. The villains tied her to the railway tracks regularly, but each time the old steam engine was about to do its deadly work we were told to come back the following Saturday. The auditorium also boasted an orchestra, and one or two nights a week Mother and Father would go dancing to the swinging music of that time.

Its wondrous attractions notwithstanding, there was menace at Britannia! It appeared in two forms: the public lavatories and the barrels of drinking water. The lavatories were situated at the side of the Pavilion. No matter how dire the need, it had been made abundantly clear to us that they were not to be used. It was equally clear that the great, green barrels marked "Cold Drinking Water" were forbidden territory. Attached to each barrel were chains that held large metal drinking cups, lined with broken white enamel.

We knew that to enter the public toilet or to touch one of those cups meant instant contact with millions of germs, which would slowly but surely, methodically and diabolically, begin our destruction. These evil, invisible forces would triumph over our strong young bodies and dread diseases would ensure our final obliteration. What these diseases were, we knew not. But we knew they existed and that their agents lurked in any toilet and water faucet outside of our own home. The lurking-germ lesson was drummed into all of us almost from day one.

By the age of six, I discovered that life held other hazards too. The shattering experience of the great fire began after a cheerful birthday party given by Mr. and Mrs. McPhail for their seven-year-old daughter, Katherine. It was a beautiful party. The next day, I returned to the McPhail house, a few doors down on Somerset, to play with Andrew, a constant chum at that time. In the third-floor playroom, Andrew and I decided to enquire by scientific experiment into how much light could be generated by burning the remnants of the birthday-cake candles.

Light streamed through uncurtained windows of the playroom, little light came from the candles, and we deemed the experiment a failure. Andrew suggested that we could produce more darkness – and hence more candle-light – in his mother's clothes closet on the second floor. He was right – especially so after his mother's nightgown caught fire. We quickly convinced each other that it would be wise to close the door, withdraw to the street, and wait to see what happened. With the clanging arrival of many "firereels" we realized with sickening suddenness that the top of the McPhail house was on fire. I decided that the only prudent course was to "opt out" of society. I headed, on the run, for what I knew to be a secure hiding place: the dog kennel behind the Doherty home. Darcy and Brian* Doherty's father had recently come from Toronto to be a minister in the government. They were my good friends. The hide-out was ideal because no one would think to look there, and the dog, though large, was kindly with children. After what seemed an interminable period of time, during which I grew steadily colder and hungrier, I knew that I would have to confront my parents. Seeking solace in the feeling that "honesty is the best policy" and "discretion the better part of valour," hungry, tired, and cold, I walked up the stairs, rang the bell, and went into our house. Father and Mother were holding an important meeting with my Mother's senior brothers.

Everybody loomed large – and seemed surprisingly pleased to see me. It seems that the police had been called and had dragged the canal for the body of one Lawrence Freiman – to no avail. I marched up to my father and said simply that I was sorry that I had burned down Mrs. McPhail's house. With relief battling chagrin, and winning, he sent me off to bed. I guess all of us were relieved at my return to society.

Other lessons in the art of living came from the inescapable bouts of childhood illness. It was considered that unless properly treated, each illness was ultimate and final. Measles was considered one of the worst and treatment was a most serious matter.

At the first suggestion of a measles rash, the small victim

---

*Brian Doherty later founded the Shaw Festival at Niagara-on-the-Lake, and Darcy became President of the Toronto Stock Exchange. He is presently Honorary Chairman of Midland Doherty Limited, stockbrokers.

22

would be confined to about ten days of darkness – all pervasive, never-ending darkness – and fed countless spoonfulls of foul-tasting medicines of mysterious origin. The belief was that exposure to any light during the measles would result in semi- or total blindness. I remember so well those dark days without end – and one moment of joy in that gloomy confinement. One evening, Mother came to say goodnight before she left to go to the Russell Theatre with Father. The door opened, and the gold lamé of her dress glimmered in the dull light from the hall. She wanted to know if I could see it well enough and if I liked it. Then she extended her sleeve to my youthful touch. Beside her, Father was equally splendid in impeccable white tie and tails. It was the custom to dress for the Russell Theatre, which boasted such fine artists as the Barrymores, the Drews, Ellen Terry, Sir John Martin Harvey, and Sarah Bernhardt. Every detail of that beautiful, brief moment is still etched clearly in my memory.

As lusty young boys are wont to do, I survived the measles and other challenges of childhood, including what was, to me, a puzzling role as the lone son between two daughters. To my older sister Dorothy I was the classic younger brother, merely tolerable at the best of times and clearly with no destiny of consequence. To my younger sister Queene I was the magical big brother, always a man in her perception. To me it was a constant perplexity as to how two sisters could regard the same me in such different lights. (I am not sure that I ever totally figured that one out.)

I even survived the mortification of accepting the fact that after repeated frustrations and failures in manual training classes I could not saw a board or hammer a nail as well as boys were supposed to be able to do. That realization, around the age of six or seven, gave me a whole new perspective. Life was fun enough but there were so very many things to be aware of, and each was a confusing mixture of benefit and of price – one paid for the benefits.

Nowhere was that fact more evident than in my mother's house.

Chapter III

My Mother's House

It would be usual to speak of 149 Somerset Street West as the home of Mr. and Mrs. A.J. Freiman, with the unspoken acknowledgement of Mr. Freiman as head of the household.

But this was Mother's house too, in a most singular way. For it was here that she performed her daily work–meeting her "clients," who came from all faiths and from all parts of Canada and elsewhere to confide, to seek, and unfailingly receive help, understanding, kindness, affection, and sound advice. Waiting in one of the drawing rooms to present their "cases" to her, the steady stream of clients created, in effect, a remarkable social clinic. And to Mother, every problem was significant, a challenge to be met and resolved.

Mother was very like Grandfather. Her eyes, like Grandfather's, shone with a promise to fulfil the needs they saw. They were eyes that brimmed with life, fun, and impulsive energy, reflecting her great love and affection for her husband, her children, and for those who came for help. Living in her house was a constant, high-spirited celebration. She was simply incapable of living any other way.

There was nothing unusual or surprising about that, for in many ways, my mother's house simply continued the way of life she had known in her parents' house. Mother was the fifth-born of Moses and Pauline Bilsky's eleven children – six daughters and five sons – more than enough to make any home a lively place. But the Bilsky home was much more than that; it was also "home" to a constant flow of visitors, Jews and non-Jews alike. For hundreds over the years, it was a place of warmth, of food, of clothing, and of love and friendship.

Interviewed in later life about her childhood, Mother was asked if the Bilskys' constant charitableness hadn't been irksome for the children.

"Good gracious no," she replied with some surprise, "it was as much the ordinary routine as going to school, eating, and going to sleep. We didn't know any other way of living. It was the usual thing when we came home from school to find that our rooms had been given to some unexpected visitor. We never knew where we were sleeping or how many of us would occupy a room. And we never knew when we went to dress what article of clothing would be missing, and it was no use having a favourite dress or hat or coat. It was sure to be given away."* That was their way of life and no one complained or even thought much about it.

Interest in people was a natural product of the Bilsky family environment, and it was natural and probably inevitable that Mother should have met Father in the way she did.

Moses Bilsky arrived home for lunch one day and announced to his family that a young man from Kingston had had the temerity to join with Moses Cramer in a house furnishings store on Rideau Street. He had the ringing name of Archibald Jacob Freiman. Daughter Lillian was intrigued, and stopped by the store a few days later to make the acquaintance of the newcomer. Not only was Archibald Jacob Freiman young, he was handsome, intelligent, and very charming. The two quickly found that they had much in common, including the same June 6 birthday, with the young merchant only five years older. Their relationship developed more as a matter of course than as a courtship, and they were married on August 18, 1903, when she was eighteen. Thus began my mother's house.

*Figler, *Lillian and Archie Freiman*, p. 16.

It is rather surprising that in my mother's time, only a generation ago, there were so few institutions for social assistance of the kind we now take for granted. It seems that few cared. At a time when there was no unemployment insurance, no baby bonusses, no OHIP, and the like, many children were hungry, they did not have shoes to go out in, or a doctor when they were ill. There was simply no money to look after them.

The institutionalizing of social assistance programs was undoubtedly one of the great advances of our society. But there have been costs beyond the dollar. In developing the "welfare state," love and kindness have progressively disappeared, giving way to an anonymity that could not be felt by those who called on Mother. She was one who cared, and that is why her work was so demanding.

Her house looked as she did. It was warm and beautiful. At first glance you didn't notice how perfectly each individual piece fit quietly into the unity of each room.

Each dinner was special, whether for the family or a large party of visiting artists, musicians, theatre people, or members of the various organizations she worked with. Large, formal dinner parties became informal under her aura of pleasant ease. I remember best the family luncheons in the main dining room when she would tell us about each of her "cases."

There was "Reb" Merle, nicknamed Reb although he was no more a rabbi than I was. He was a small man with a straggly, greying beard, a crumpled black hat, and a long, worn, black coat. I can still hear him yell as he sat on the seat of his cart, pulled by a horse as old and tired as himself: "Rags, bones, and bottles." My mother's service was to provide this "client" with a new horse each time one expired. I never did understand how so many horses could die so often, but apparently Reb Merle asked her to buy only old horses because they were less expensive. I think he also had a greater affection for old horses than for young ones. So Mother arranged for each new old horse, and Reb Merle went about his rags, bones, and bottles business. Whenever I saw him in the synagogue he always inquired about her with the kindliest light in his aging eyes.

I remember, too, the case of the wizened, anaemic-looking little man who wept to my mother that his wife, an extremely large woman, beat him unmercifully. He showed Mother the great black-and-blue bruises that resulted from these unpleasant encounters. His case clearly called for outside help.

The biggest cop on the force was Bill Cowan. Irish, with blond-red hair, he weighed over 300 pounds and stood six-foot-five. Our chauffeur Eddie drove Mother and the little man to the corner of Rideau and Sussex Streets, where Officer Cowan was directing traffic. Calling him over for a small consultation, Mother explained the situation to Officer Cowan and invited him to join her in the car. They drove to the large lady's house where Bill, drawing himself up to his full size, warned her that if she ever beat up the little man again, the same fate would befall her. With lower lip protruding, Officer Cowan threatened, "If you touch him again, I'll knock your head off, and for good measure arrest you for assault and battery." The case was settled.

Then there was the malodorous lady. She arrived one day to inform Mother that, regrettably, her son was being held by the Montreal police. She was hesitant about relating the full story, but slowly the facts emerged as Mother inquired more deeply.

The woman's son had been apprehended by the police after he had broken into a small store. This was regrettable. But even more regrettable, he had shot the proprietor through the head when interrupted while taking money from the cash register. Under repeated questioning the woman revealed that, most regrettably, he had been found guilty of murder and had been sentenced to hang.

Whatever the facts of the case, Mother, confronted by a woman weeping helplessly over her son's fate, decided that something must be done. She promised to prove to the authorities that the death sentence should not be permitted to stand. Mother also decided that the lady should stay in our home because she needed kindness and attention during this time. After a few days, my father rebelled. Not only was the lady malodorous, but his nose told him that now the whole house smelled. He tried to convince Mother that the lady would be more comfortable, and he certainly would be, if he made arrangements for her at the Chateau Laurier, the city's largest hotel. Mother would not hear of such a proposal. She was adamant, believing that the poor woman should not be left alone. Naturally, she stayed on.

As promised, Mother made representation on behalf of the

young man to the Cabinet through the Minister of Justice. Within a few weeks she received a letter from the minister. She was so nervous she handed it to me, unopened, saying, "Lawrence, I can't open this. You read it." The sentence had been commuted to life imprisonment. I recall so well the poor woman sobbing on her knees and kissing Mother's hands in thankfulness. Mother told her to go to her room to rest. Within an hour she reappeared saying, plaintively, "Mrs. Freiman, I now have only one more favour. When are you going to get my son out of jail?"

One of Mother's most dramatic cases involved war. A telephone call came one morning when Mother was quite ill. Her caller stated that three young men who had deserted from the enemy army early in the First World War had been interned in Canada, and were being returned to their country that night on a ship sailing at midnight from Quebec. The caller appealed to her to get them off the ship because they would be executed for their desertion as soon as they were returned and in the hands of the authorities.

At lunch Mother informed Dad that she was going to Quebec to get them off the ship. He remonstrated with her, trying to convince her that the only rational way to deal with this matter was through the Department of Immigration in Ottawa. Mother argued that her experience in these matters had been that Ottawa could not move with the required speed. She would have to go to Quebec immediately to do something. "I must catch the 3:00 train to Quebec City and somehow get those boys off the ship before it sails," she said firmly. Her feeling of urgency was so great that hurrying to leave the house she slipped on the marble floor of the foyer, hit her head on a radiator, and fainted. The bump on her head was not the greatest of my mother's health concerns at that time, however. A long-standing heart condition was worsening steadily. Ill as she was, she caught the train to Quebec and reached the dock barely an hour before the ship was to sail. There, a soldier, with rifle, was marching up and down in front of the gangplank. He saw Mother's Great War Veterans' Badge* and recognized her as the only woman in Canada at that

*The Great War Veterans' Association was the forerunner of the Canadian Legion. Mother, who helped found it, was one of its first honorary members.

28

time who wore this badge. With considerable surprise he inquired, "What are you doing here at this hour, Mrs. Freiman?" Mother told him and asked what authority she would require, and from whom, to have the men removed from the ship. The soldier called the senior ranking officer, a lieutenant-colonel. Mother repeated her questions and was told that if she could obtain an order from the Minister of Justice in Ottawa the three men could be taken off the ship. It was 11:15.

It was well-known that the Minister of Justice did not suffer late-night telephone calls gladly. Mother resolutely placed the call, and without preamble stated flatly that she was not asking the minister to release the three men from the ship—she was demanding that he do so immediately.

"In the event that these men are not removed from that ship," she said, "I will hold you, as Minister of Justice, and the Canadian government, guilty of murder." She said that she would accept any financial responsibility, gave her personal bond for the good conduct of the boys, and promised that she would help them find suitable employment. Out-gunned and somewhat overwhelmed, the minister granted her request. Minutes later, the astonished men were removed from the ship. They caught the midnight train to Ottawa.

The next morning I came down to breakfast to see her with three relieved, smiling guests.

There often seemed to be a large measure of intuition in Mother's actions. Once, she "knew" that the wife of a reporter for one of the Ottawa newspapers was going to have a baby. I met him some years later at a Wartime Information Board dinner in Washington, D.C., where he told me the story. In the Depression days he made only $18 a week as a reporter, which certainly did not permit any fancy "extras" for a new baby. He and his wife were naturally delighted when an entire layette arrived, but were totally astonished at how Mother could have known about the impending birth. Neither of them had seen Mother for some time and, in fact, scarcely knew her.

But Mother did know, and having found a complete layette, which included everything from diaper pins to dressing table, she bought it without inquiring about the price. On the card that accompanied the layette she had written two words: "With love."

When Father got the bill, along with several others for things Mother had bought for other people, he inquired, "What is this? Who ordered all these baby things? And all these other things for so many people?"

Mother said firmly, "I did it, and I'm glad I did."

It was one of the very few times that their always lively discussions came close to a fight. I remember Dad taking a plate from the dining room table and smashing it on the floor. When Mother countered by doing the same, they started to laugh – fight over. She patiently explained everything – except how she knew about the baby's arrival.

Mother's house was never fuller than during the war years. I found one day that my bedroom had been expropriated by a large group of ladies making bandages and knitting warm gloves, scarves, and socks for the soldiers, "the boys in the trenches." Gone were my toy soldiers, punching bag and games, all replaced by sewing machines, chairs, and the good women.

There was so much to do – and Mother seemed involved in all of it. There were work groups and societies to be organized, funds to be raised for war auxiliary programs. I can vaguely remember bingo games and auctions and sales being held to assist the wives and children of soldiers who had been killed or were missing in action. And there were the "boys" from the army camps around Ottawa who came to our house for the Jewish holidays. We placed mattresses and blankets in the billiard room and all through the living rooms. The "boys" slept there and attended synagogue before leaving for overseas. When they left, others came. When the long casualty lists arrived we knew many who would not be coming back.

The contagion of war in Europe came to North America in the form of a massive influenza outbreak in 1918. News of the epidemic, and a plea for Mother's help, came to our house on a Friday night. After prayers to begin the Sabbath, and during the dinner that followed, she was called to the telephone. It was Mayor Harold Fisher calling to ask if she could come to City Hall immediately to assist with an emergency. Because it was the Sabbath evening she would not be driven, but walked on this cold, snowy night to the mayor's office. There she learned that the influenza was more virulent and widespread than anyone had suspected. There were not nearly enough doctors, hospital beds, ambulances – or hearses. When Mother was asked to be the emergency administrator and take full charge, she replied, "Yes, of course."

For days she did not return home, working endless hours, taking but a few hours' rest on a chesterfield in the mayor's office. In time, the epidemic was under control and she was home again with her family and "clients," coping as usual with new crises and out of the ordinary developments.

Eventually came Armistice Day – November 11, 1918. For me, a boy of nine, it meant being awakened at 5:00 in the morning, bundled into the car decorated with lots of Union Jacks, and given a big washtub to bang in the cacophony of church bells ringing and of thousands cheering to celebrate that great moment.

But peace did not mean the end of all problems. Of special concern was the well-being and future of thousands of Ukrainian war orphans. When it became apparent to Mother that the international committees organized to resolve the problem had not achieved anything meaningful, she decided to do something. In New York a People's Relief Committee had been formed to raise funds to bring as many Jewish orphans as possible from the Ukraine. Professor Elie Heifetz of the Ukraine who had organized the committee in New York came to Canada to seek support. Mother helped organize a meeting of delegates from all over Canada at the Chateau Laurier in Ottawa, October 6 to 8, 1920. The Jewish War Orphans of Canada Committee was formed to find Canadian foster homes for some of the Ukrainian children. Mother was appointed National President and Dad was named Chairman of the executive committee. Mrs. Arthur Meighen, wife of the Prime Minister, became Honorary President. Honorary Vice-Presidents were Lady Mortimer Davis, Lady Borden, wife of Sir Robert Borden, and Mrs. Mark Workman. She and her husband were eminent Montreal philanthropists.

So began for Mother one of her greatest adventures.

In that jet looo era she travelled in trains across Canada from coast to coast, telling people about the children and their needs. She visited homes of people who wished to be foster parents, in order to ensure that the children would be well looked after. And finally she organized a group to go overseas to arrange for the children to come to Canada.

The organizing group sailed from Quebec on February 5, 1921. In Europe the situation was complicated. There were many thousands of children needing help and arrangements could be made for only about 150 of them to come to Canada.

It wasn't until August that arrangements had finally been completed for the children's journey. Mother, accompanied by her cousin Nellie Pierce, a member of the executive committee, left immediately for Europe. Their first meeting with the children was one of the most emotional episodes in Mother's life. On the Friday night before sailing for Canada, the large silver Kiddush cup was filled with wine and passed among the children during the Sabbath service. The children heard in the moment of blessing something as old as the beginnings of our people, "Blessed art thou, O Lord our God, King of the universe, who hast sanctified us by thy commandments and hast taken pleasure in us, and in love and favour hast given us thy holy Sabbath as an inheritance, a memorial of the creation. . . . For thou hast chosen us and sanctified us. . ."

The children sailed for their new homes on the *S.S. Scandinavia.* When they arrived in Quebec they were greeted by their new Canadian foster parents and several hundred others who were deeply touched by the event. The first to race up the gangplank was Dad, clasping Mother and twelve-year-old Gladys in one giant bear hug. Gladys would be part of the family for more than a dozen years, until she married and settled in Toronto. Cousin Nellie took her new son Michael to her home in Montreal, as did other foster parents their children to homes throughout the country. The rewards of that gratifyingly successful project continue to this day.

At this time there were other complicated immigration problems. The federal government passed an order-in-council restricting immigration of various groups who were applying for admission. Several hundred Jews from eastern Europe, fleeing the ravages of war and fearing further anti-Semitic pogroms,

32

arrived in Halifax—to find that they could not get off the boat. The legislation that prevented their admission had been passed after they left Europe. One of these immigrants, David Rome, who became a distinguished scholar and historian wrote:

> Halifax, Winter 1921. In a large dark hall some 500 Jewish men and women were herded together, victims of red tape.
>
> Then she came to see her Jews. The preparations were those made for a king about to visit a prison. There were whisperings and scrubbings and preenings and warnings.
>
> The evening came. The immigrants gathered in the large hall, with dark, hopeless, sallow faces. But Mrs. Freiman was from Canada. She was accustomed to seeing people straight and well and proud and healthy. Before the reality of her cases she almost broke down herself. She wanted to say something, but these people could not understand English and her Yiddish was less than limited. She put her motherly arms about the two or three closest to her and comforted them, "nesht vein, nesht vein" (don't weep). Her vocabulary gave out and she kept repeating these words, "nesht vein, nesht vein."[*]

Mother and Father intervened with the Department of Immigration, working tirelessly to bring about a review of the case of each immigrant. After a token number of permits were issued, disappointed but not defeated, they managed to make arrangements with the Cuban government for the majority of the immigrants to go there. But for Mother and Father, that solution was a shallow compromise and a bitterly disappointing blot on Canada's reputation. They did not know then that the blot would grow even larger.

I was by this time deeply involved in the matters that concerned my mother's house; it could not have been otherwise, given the extremely close bonds between us. And while many of those matters were serious and worrisome, our life was by no means all sombre seriousness.

When I had completed high school and moved to Montreal to

*Figler, *Lillian and Archie Freiman*, pp. 74-75.

attend McGill University, I telephoned Mother virtually every day – reversing the charges, of course. In those days I drove a red Stutz roadster, complete with blonde, pretty girls, and fancied myself quite the man around campus. But everyone knew that I had no time for anyone whenever Mother came to visit me. She was such fun, and she loved to go dancing. So we did on every possible occasion. Fortunately, the girls understood. Even years later, after I had married and brought my wife Audrey back to Ottawa, I still went to have breakfast with Mother almost every day, just to be with her. Happily, Audrey, too, understood the bonds between my mother and me. I know now, of course, that throughout her life, Mother was a rare and truly remarkable woman. Yet never was there any feeling of awe or timidity in my relationship with her. From my earliest memory she was simply Mother, warm and loving, and loved and respected. Her family, her children, were most important in her life, and no matter how busy she was with her countless other activities, the family came first. We all knew that and, I suppose, took it rather for granted, because our love was so deep and unquestioning.

During the decade of the thirties, the lightness of our days was in painful contrast to the sadness we felt for so many who were refused admittance into Canada. With the advent of Hitler's Nazi Germany, new wanderers began their search for new homes. They carried their few possessions, hoping to find sanctuary. Applications for admission to Canada streamed in throughout the 1930s, but the approvals were so few that Mother's face was often very dark in those years. When thousands or even hundreds of thousands of people could have been saved by our country from death in the concentration camps and the gas chambers, Canada's door was practically closed. Looking back, it seems incredible to see the small trickle of Jewish immigrants who arrived during the critical pre-war years when emigration for them was still possible. We must assume that the figures below include Jews coming into Canada from countries other than those oppressed by the Nazis; therefore, the numbers of Jews who were saved are even fewer than these numbers suggest.

1933	.781
1934	.869
1935	.803
1936	.659
1937	.559
1938.	.748*

Mother bore the pain of her own advancing illness, along with the agony of knowing that each time there was a rejection of immigration it could well mean death in the Nazi machine. She knew, and we knew, what the Canadian government seemingly did not want to know. I tried to help her in this frustrating, complicated work with the Department of Immigration and listened with disbelief to excuses as our officials became bogged down in their sterile regulations and red tape.

A poignant drama occurred in Ottawa when an eminent Jewish doctor from Berlin, who had been a colonel in the German army during the First World War, came to seek permission to immigrate. He told my mother what had happened to his daughter. She had been placed by her teacher on a stool in front of the class. The teacher directed a pointer to the child's eyes and said to the class, "'You see these eyes? They are Jew eyes; they see only evil.' Then, he pointed to her nose. 'You see this nose? It is a Jew nose. It smells only evil. You see this Jew mouth? It speaks only evil.'"

The doctor told us this story coldly, almost clinically. His daughter's humiliation was not as horrible, however, as Canada's rejection of his application to immigrate. The doctor returned to Nazi Germany to a fate that only God now knows.

The desperation to come to Canada and the supreme endurance of those seeking sanctuary was shown by an old rabbi and his group of about 150 students from the Warsaw Yeshiva, a school of religious learning. They literally walked or took trains and buses all the way from Warsaw to eventually reach Tokyo. But they arrived just before war with Japan began, so they were

*From Statistics Canada, *Canada Yearbook.*

destined to stay there. Sometimes subsistence meant an apple a day. But they did endure. Just after the war the rabbi arrived in Ottawa to try for their admission to Canada.

A few of us met with Mr. Crerar, the Minister of Immigration at that time. He said he would "settle" for about half their total number. "Mr. Crerar," I told him, "although I am a merchant, I do not wish to be an agent for the sale or purchase of Jewish lives at half price." This led to a more frank discussion, and at the end of the meeting the minister recognized the human principle involved and admitted the entire group.

While much of Mother's work was for Jewish causes, there was nothing sectarian about her continuing concern for human principles. Mother identified herself with women's liberation long before it became a movement. She worked for a day nursery so that women could leave their children well cared for while they went to work. With Mother Superior Mary Thomas Aquinas, Mother helped build the Joan of Arc Institute for "wayward girls," as they were called in those days when "the way" was rather more narrow than it is today. Girls who did not have jobs, girls from reform institutions, and unmarried girls who were pregnant, were all welcomed and aided there. When the babies of these girls were born they could be adopted with the help of the mother superior and the sisters. Mother also worked for a home training centre for domestic workers, who were generally paid little and treated very badly. She wanted to provide training so that they could earn better wages and work in better conditions. She worked for homes for elderly women, to help them attain a greater dignity and a better way of life in these later years.

Her days were full of countless concerns for people–and there was always more to be done "for the boys who had served." With her friend, the late Colonel Eddie Baker, whose work for the blind earned him a special place in Canadian history, she helped institute Poppy Day, so that poppies could be made by blind veterans and the funds used by them. When the Honours List was reinstituted on January 1, 1934, she received the award of Officer of the Order of the British Empire. She also received the Vimy Medal. I was with her in hospital the day it arrived from Lieutenant-Colonel R. de la Bruyère Girouard. Vimy Ridge was one of the First World War battles where Canadian losses were tremendous. In memory of this battle a monument was erected by the Government of Canada in 1936. Veterans from Canada and officials from France, England, and Belgium made a pilgrimage to Vimy. To mark the occasion one hundred medals were struck. With the medal, Colonel Girouard enclosed the following notation:

> The enclosed Vimy medal is one of 100 presentation medals struck for presentation to deserving persons in France, England, and Belgium. As quartermaster for the pilgrimage (from Canada) I had much pleasure in bringing this one for you who by your devotion, interest, and work in the welfare of ex-soldiers more than deserves to be remembered among the highest. 3-9-36.

Mother's illness was taking an increasingly harsh toll. She suffered more and was confined to home and bed for longer and longer periods. Even so, I remember her bounding out of bed whenever she felt a release from pain. Although these times were brief she continued her work. The telephone by her bedside rang constantly. Everything to which she devoted her life continued.

At the early age of fifty-five my mother's tireless efforts took their final toll. She died in Montreal's Royal Victoria Hospital on November 4, 1940. Although our faith requires early burial, the demand by "her people" in Montreal to pay their respects was so great that the requirement could not be observed. In a small Jewish undertaking establishment in the humble St. Urbain district, thousands came to pay tribute to her. In Ottawa, again, the tribute was repeated, one of the largest in the history of the city, complete with a military guard of honour.

For two full days, a steady line of people passed her coffin, covered with a blanket of poppies, made especially by blind veterans. There was a particularly moving moment when I noticed in the line our old friend Reb Merle reciting the Hebrew prayer of mourning. At that moment, directly behind him, in full dress uniform, was General LaFlèche, then Deputy Minister of

National Defence, who came to a halt and saluted. It was a touching tribute to a life of work and love that would be remembered for generations.

Mother's pride in Judaism, and her unswerving conviction that there would one day be a Jewish state of freedom and dignity inspired her work for Hadassah, the institution she started and helped develop until it was one of the most significant women's organizations in Canada.

In Israel stands an agricultural school for girls called Nahalal, meaning "another one." Nahalal stands today as a tribute to my mother's inspiration, the work of Canadian Hadassah, and to the love and inspiration of its remarkable director, Hannah Meisel Schochet.

At a memorial service in Tel Aviv on November 18, 1940, just two weeks after mother's death, Golda Meir, the indomitable former leader of Israel, spoke of Mother:

> She was a symbol of what a proud Jewish woman should be. She did not work out of sympathy to suffering Jews but because the sorrow and tragedies of our people became her personal sorrows, and therefore she had to solve them. I have seen her in Palestine, overwhelmed with joy over the accomplishments and criticizing what to her seemed mistakes. But her criticism, too, was not to mistakes that others had made, but as though she, too, was responsible for them. I have seen her among her friends and co-workers in Canada – the idol of all Canadian Jewry. I have seen her master difficult problems within the Canadian Zionist movement and Hadassah with the tact, wisdom, and above all love for human beings which was so characteristic of her.
>
> ...And I have seen her in her home surrounded by her fine family that worshipped her. Often have I seen her ill in bed under strict orders of her physician, but never for a moment was she resting from her work.
>
> ...Her fine, deep understanding of Zionism and her desire that the Jewish home in Palestine shall be built on the principle of justice....Because she carried her Jewishness with such dignity and pride she was so beloved and respected also by the non-Jewish community in Canada.

The Jewish people, the Zionist movement, have lost one of their dearest daughters and co-workers. And this at a time when tragedy and destruction envelops the majority of our nation. This at a time when we are so in need of people who are not merely prepared to help but of people whose souls are delicately tuned to our sufferings. . .

There was something prophetic in Mrs. Meir's last statement. Israel is now facing such a serious moment, and more than ever has the "need of people who are not merely prepared to help but of people whose souls are delicately tuned to our sufferings."

It was this "delicate tuning" to the sufferings of all people that made my mother's house the remarkable place that it was—and that provided one of the strong pillars that supported my father's house.

> Only the light of these your days,
> Only the warmth of these your deeds,
> Eternal sunshine from them speeds,
> About them sunshine ever plays!

> —from "In Memoriam," written for Lillian Freiman by
> A.M. Klein

Chapter IV

In My Father's House... there are many mansions

On a Saturday night, near the end of my public school days, I glimpsed for the first time one of the most important of the many mansions in my father's house.

During those young, carefree days, Father would sometimes, if my conduct during the week had been judged satisfactory, take me to the early evening show at Loewe's Capitol Theatre.

Built in the movie palace tradition of the 1920s, Loewe's seated over 2,000 and had massive ersatz marble columns everywhere. The ceiling offered the incongruous divinity of countless angels under great blue-white clouds, clustered around a muscle-bound nude male angel blowing an extremely long, thin trumpet.

The show contained all of the wonders of vaudeville, plus a feature film, a cartoon, and the news. There were six vaudeville acts. The first was always the acrobats, who fascinated me with their strength, skill, and daring. They were usually followed by the stand-up comic or a dancer with straw hat and cane, who often told jokes during his dancing. There were musicians, girl dancers, and all the other glorious people that made up this wondrous world of vaudeville.

This particular Saturday evening the vaudeville program had already begun when we arrived. Catastrophe struck during the comedian's act. After only a few minutes of the performance my father announced, "We are leaving now!" I was stunned, for leaving then meant that I would not see the other vaudeville acts, the cartoon, the news, or the feature film.

As we left I asked Dad why. He was surprised that I did not know. The little man on stage was the typical Minsky-type, Jewish-caricature-comedian of that period. Dad explained that this so-called comedian exhibited total vulgarity in his attempts to amuse small minds by ridiculing a proud people. He said that no Jew with any pride should witness such a crude and distasteful exhibition.

As we walked home, he spoke of Palestine when, one day, even though he might not live to see it, there would be a Jewish state. He said that with this state, there would be a regeneration of Jewish culture and a new pride, a pride that would drive the type of vulgarian we had just seen from the stages of the world. The little man with the bowler hat pulled over his ears, the exaggerated, false, hooked nose, and the ill-fitting suit would be replaced by prestigious artists in the performing arts, by fine dancing, good music, and worthy drama. Years later, as I listened to the Israel Symphony performing on the same stage where we had seen the comedian, I realized the truth of Dad's prophecy. The comic, and his ilk, had been driven off by artists such as Leonard Bernstein, Jerome Robbins, Isaac Stern, Richard Tucker, Jan Peerce, and countless others.

What had started as a "fun night out" with Father became for me the first realization of how vitally important the fact and the concept of the Jewish nation was in my father's house. He and Mother worked tirelessly to that end, labouring unceasingly across Canada, abroad, and at home in Ottawa with the many distinguished visitors who came from around the world to meet and plan and discuss.

I recall the early visits of Dr. Chaim Weizmann, whom my father always addressed in letters as "My dear chief." He sometimes came with his attractive wife, Vera—I still remember how elegant she was with her long cigarette holder and her chic dresses. Although her features were not beautiful, her strength of character and brilliance shone through her sparkling eyes. As for Dr. Weizmann, anyone who knew him remembered his lined face and his furrowed brow that bespoke the suffering and travail of our people. And yet there was his great humour, splendid courage, and wisdom – and his love of being with young people.

Shmaryahu Levin, the great conversationalist and Zionist lecturer in Hebrew, Yiddish, Russian, German, and English, visited too, as did Nahum Sokolow, the great collaborator of Dr. Weizmann in the diplomatic activities that led to the Balfour Declaration in 1917. Yitzchak Ben-Zvi also came to our house. He later succeeded Dr. Weizmann, to become the second President of Isreal.

When I met Ben-Zvi again, while leading the first Canadian mission to Israel with Samuel Bronfman in 1960, he smilingly recalled visiting Dad in his office at the store and his difficulty in finding the stairway to Father's third-floor office.

One year, Menahem Mendel Ussishkin spent nearly a month at Meach Lake, our summer home in Quebec. He was a strong, burly, gruff man who had a tremendous will and total determination. His purpose as President of the Jewish National Fund was to buy any land that was available from the Arabs, at any price. He believed that unbought land would have to be paid for later in Jewish blood. One night after dinner he stretched out on the couch for a short siesta. Seeing that he was without a pillow, my sister Dorothy thoughtfully went upstairs and brought one down. She carefully placed it under his head, saying quietly, "I hope you will be more comfortable."

"You might have thought of this when I first stretched out for my rest," he countered, his smile belying the gruffness of his voice and words.

Vladimir Jabotinsky, the rebel and great orator, also came. Although Father could not have disagreed more with any Jewish thinker in the world than he did with Jabotinsky, he welcomed him. It was a personal requirement of Dad's to try and understand every side of a problem. If there was disagreement, he searched people's minds for a resolution. Nachum Goldmann came too, with his incisive intellect, startling brilliance, and fine humour – all exquisitely expressed. And there were so many more. They were the generation of the first Zionist Congress in

Basle, Switzerland, in 1897, where political Zionism began. They worked constantly over many years in the political struggle that led to the establishment of the State of Israel because they recognized the need to make Zionism a world movement. With that purpose they travelled and convinced those who would listen to join them.

They were all motivated by the same compelling belief, a belief that Father enunciated so succinctly during an interview a short time before he died.

> To be a Zionist means to dream of a great Jewish homeland, to tie oneself spiritually and morally with the glorious Jewish past, with the prophets, philosophers, thinkers, with the Yehuda Halevigs, the Rambams, the Herzls, the Pinskers, and A'had Ha'am, with their great contribution to the culture and soul of the Jewish people. To be a Zionist means to believe in Jewish history, in Palestine and in the God of Israel.

The United States, the United Kingdom, and, progressively, Canada, supported the concept of Israel. It was not long before the international visitors arrived in our home from England, the United States, and South Africa. Louis Lipsky, President of the Zionist Organization came from America. From England we met Simon Marks, later Lord Marks, and Sir Montague Burton. This was inspiring company indeed for a man whose life in Canada started—at age thirteen—in a grade 1 classroom where everyone except him spoke English.

Archibald Jacob Freiman was born in the small village of Wirballen, Lithuania in 1880. He studied with his grandfather, the gaon, or "rabbi's rabbi," of that district, remaining with him until his Bar Mitzvah, a few years after his father emigrated to Hamilton, Ontario. In 1893, this tall, slender European boy of thirteen arrived in Hamilton to join his father. In Europe, he had been absorbing the great wisdom of his grandfather, studying, at advanced levels, religion and related subjects. In Hamilton he was assigned to a grade 1 class to learn English, and spent his first days practising "cat, rat, and hat." The experience was so humiliating that he was determined to do whatever was necessary to get it over with as soon as possible. Working day and night, he not only became completely fluent in English, but completed the entire grade-school course in two years, graduating from grade 8 at the age of fifteen. Then he attended Hamilton Business College, graduating two years later—"ready for the world"—at seventeen.

In the Horatio Alger tradition of the day, he left for Gardner, Massachusetts, where his father had made arrangements with a cousin who owned a small men's store. Father received room and board and $2 a week. He boasted years later that he always managed to save something out of his weekly pay. Gardner was a small factory town, with most people working shifts. It was therefore good business to be open when the shifts came off. Dad was in the shop at 6:30 every morning and stayed until whatever hour of the night people stopped coming in.

After two years in Gardner, Dad left for Kingston, Ontario. But he decided that Kingston was not the place where he wanted to establish business. He went to Ottawa because he thought it a beautiful city and one in which he wanted to live. I remember him telling me, "Look around you, son. You see, I was right in coming here."

In Ottawa, he met an "older" man, Moses Cramer, a merchant in his early forties. Dad, then twenty, felt that he could benefit from the older man's experience in business. He borrowed $500 from his father and went into partnership with Mr. Cramer. They opened the Canada House Furnishing Company in 1899, three blocks east of where Freiman's was to be on Rideau Street.

Dad's first store was a home furnishing store specializing in draperies and carpets. It prospered as he and his partner became closer friends and good business colleagues. Then a problem arose—in the form of Mrs. Cramer. She treated my father as a child, which, considering his young age, was probably understandable. But within three years, Father had had enough. He negotiated another loan from his father and established the Archibald J. Freiman Department Store, at 73 Rideau Street, opening the doors for the first time in 1903. In starting his own business with borrowed money, Dad discovered that he had acquired a new partner. His father proceeded to move himself and his family to Ottawa in order to watch his investment.

This new partner proved to be somewhat difficult. Grand-

44

father was imperious and demanding. As the senior Freiman, he felt that his critique of every situation was not only an essential part of each day, but an absolute necessity if Dad was to develop as a businessman. Father was young, aggressive, bright, and ambitious; Grandfather taciturn and critical. Father did the work; Grandfather supervised and found fault. The partnership was clearly doomed. The final break came when Grandfather had criticized so much of the buying that Father refused to buy any more. Buying was too undignified for Grandfather, so the store began to run out of goods.

In 1917, Dad decided to buy out his father's interest. His bank from the beginning had been the Standard Bank of Canada, which had been acquired by the Canadian Imperial Bank of Commerce. Father went to the bank's head office in Toronto to tell the president of the progress of the business and what he wanted to do. Grandfather now wanted a substantial amount for his small original investment. Dad assured the bank president, Mr. Logan, that if the bank would advance enough to buy out his father's interest, he would build the largest department store in Ottawa. The president rang for his secretary, the cheque was made out on the spot, and Father was launched as an independent businessman.

Despite the strains of the partnership, the business had done well. Father was only thirty-three years of age when we moved to the fine house on Somerset Street and established a way of life that never changed thereafter.

He prospered as a merchant for many reasons: partly because he was in the right place at the right time; partly because he was keenly attuned to the needs and tastes of people, and knew how to satisfy them; partly because he was a sound manager of money–and mostly because he loved every aspect of the business he was in. Merchandising for him was endlessly exciting, and even the periods of severe strain and problems, of economic ups and downs, never dulled that sense of involvement and adventure.

Father liked the grand manner, and it came to full flower a few years after the move to Somerset Street when he established a country home at Meach Lake, fourteen miles north of Ottawa in the Gatineau Hills.

Meach Lake is a four-and-a-half mile jewel of clear water surrounded by rolling green hills. The country home was known as Meach Lake, although Mother and Dad called it "Mizpah" ("the lookout" in Hebrew), and was located on one of the highest hills. From the terrace we could see for many miles beyond the lake and those soft, sloping hills. On one side of the terrace there was a large fireplace. The house had an entrance road of about a half mile, with gardens that led to the house. In all, the estate had 525 acres. The house was of granite, softened by latticework. Inside there were spacious drawing rooms and there were twelve bedrooms. Equally ample were the garage and chauffeur's quarters above, with a hall, two bedrooms, living room, and kitchen. It was all gloriously grand.

Father now had his business, his health and vigour, his noble wife, and three children. But he had much more. He shared the adventure of our people working to establish a national homeland that would bring new pride and dignity to Jews wherever they lived.

Father was twelve when the Dreyfus case occurred in France. He was sixteen when Dr. Herzl published his *Judenstadt*, and seventeen when the Zionist Congress was convened in 1897 by Dr. Herzl. At twenty-one Father attended the second convention of the Federation of Zionist Societies in Montreal during 1901. In 1919, he became Chairman of the societies' executive committee and was elected President in 1921, when the Jews of the world were already faced with the aftermath of the two-sided Balfour Declaration, a statement that spoke of establishing a Jewish national home, but at the same time made establishment impossible by preserving land-possession rights of the Arabs. If Zionism was to work, there had to be an understanding of, and material contribution to, what Israel meant. To this end he set his heart and mind.

In those early days he was convinced that the British government intended, through the Balfour Declaration, to establish a Jewish State. He was happy that other countries were showing support for the pledge of the new homeland. The Senate of the United States adopted a resolution endorsing it, and approval was also given by France and Italy. In Ottawa my grandfather, Moses Bilsky, tall and proud at eighty-eight, led a "monster" parade when the mandate for Palestine was announced in 1917. Later, Ottawa's pioneer Jew held the hand of his eight-year-old grandson, and the parade continued to the Rideau Street synagogue, where, although it was a weekday, a service of thanksgiving was held.

But it was not long until the first fallout came from the dual British policy. In the White Paper of 1922, Great Britain declared that its mandate in Palestine would no longer apply to TransJordan, thereby reducing the promised Jewish homeland to one-third of the size anticipated. Jewish immigration would be tied to the number of people the land could support, a judgement totally controlled by the Mandatory Power.

It was during this period that Zionism began to be a potent force in Canada.

In 1927, Menahem Mendel Ussishkin, President of the Jewish National Fund, came to Ottawa on an important mission – to persuade Father and Mother, and through them the Canadian Zionist Organization, to purchase some 46,000 dunams (about 11,000 acres) of land on the coastal plain not far from Tel Aviv.

Father agreed that the matter should be put before the Zionist convention, to be held later that year in Winnipeg. The land in question was a vast sand wasteland known to the Arabs as Wadi Hawareth and in biblical times as Emek Hepher. The land had dramatic meaning in Jewish history, which Ussishkin evoked at the Winnipeg convention:

Joshua had conquered Emek Hepher from a Canaanite king and gave it to the tribe of Menasseh. The Zekala, a tribe of Cretan pirates related to the Philistines, occupied it until it was liberated a second time in the wars of Deborah, Saul, and David. King Solomon made it into a separate province of Dor and appointed his son-in-law as governor (Kings: 4-10, 11). In the days of the second temple King Sidon of Phoenicia took possession of the plain, but it was liberated by the Hasmondans under King Alexander Jannaeus.

With the destruction of the second temple and the fall of Judea this area again fell into non-Jewish hands. After the lapse of 2,000 years the time had come for it to be redeemed a fourth time. Shall it be now, in the year one thousand, nine hundred and twenty-seven? Shall the name of Canadian Jews be inscribed in the new Jewish chronicles as having redeemed this area? Has the wheel of history again come to a full cycle?*

That day, the answer was given. The convention authorized $1,000,000 to purchase the land. And so it happened that the Emek was reclaimed for the fourth time. I remember, on my first trip to Palestine in 1934, seeing the vast stretches of sand, spotted here and there by clumps of long, yellow grass. Within two decades Emek Hepher had been transformed into a lush garden of green trees, small sparkling lakes, orange and grapefruit groves, towns and villages. It became the breadbasket for Tel Aviv, a home for farmers and workers, and a significant food base for Israel. Two villages mark the boundaries of the long, narrow Emek. One – Havazelet Hasharon** – is named after Mother; the other – Bet Aharon† – is named for Father. Linked by the land in seeming caress, the towns are precious memorials to our family and to Canadian Zionism in the history of Israel.

Despite the agonizingly slow progress toward Jewish statehood, Father had faith in British institutions and believed that the Mandatory Power would meet its obligations. His many speeches indicated an unwavering trust – until 1929, when the Arab riots and massacres in Hebrun and other Jewish centres devastated Jewish life and security. The Royal Commission, appointed by Britain to investigate the riots, relieved the Arabs of blame. In October 1930, Lord Passfield issued his White Paper. Its main thrust was to restrict even further the immigration of Jews into Palestine. Father's faith in the British approach was shattered, and he took the offensive, pleading for the purchase of more land and organizing campaigns for funds to finance it. In a statement of protest against the Passfield Paper, my father declared:

> It is true that our task is similar to that of our ancestors in the days of Pharaoh when told to make bricks without straw being given to them. For we are told to build a national home

*Figler, *Lillian and Archie Freiman*, p. 231.
**Lily of the Valley in Hebrew.
†House of Aharon (Aharon being Father's Hebrew name).

48

without immigration or the right to acquire land. But even such seemingly insurmountable difficulties we will overcome.

The Jewish will has never faltered and so with perseverance and the help of God we will obtain our goal.

In February 1931, a new storm broke, one that threatened to divide Zionists the world over. The storm was caused by the public release of a letter from Premier MacDonald to Dr. Weizmann that purported to remove "certain misconceptions and misunderstandings" about British policy in Palestine. Couched in friendly terms, the letter attempted to explain away certain passages of the anti-Zionist Passfield White Paper, which had been denounced not only by Jews but also by leading British statesmen of all parties. After receiving the letter, Dr. Weizmann issued a statement to the effect that it had re-established the basis of co-operation with the Mandatory Power.

That April, at the first Ontario Zionist Regional Conference, Edward E. Gelber, Chairman of the Resolutions Committee, read a resolution that would accept the MacDonald letter as a basis for further negotiations with the Mandatory Power.

My Father interjected: "The Jews of Canada will never accept the MacDonald letter as a compensation for the Passfield White Paper. As long as the Passfield Paper has not been entirely recalled, we cannot speak of negotiations. The MacDonald letter is merely a whitewash for Passfield."*

The conference agreed, and the resolution was defeated. Father's strength of principle, and firmness on that and all issues, did much to cement and strengthen the Zionist movement.

In the frightening years of the 1930s, when Naziism was gaining support, the world did not recognize that Hitler's venemous anti-Semitism had in fact become an international scourge of the Jewish people. Hitler had sympathizers throughout the western world, among whom were Sir Oswald Mosley in England and Pierre Laval in France. It was inevitable that this ugliness would find its way to Canada. In Montreal, anti-Semitic rallies were

*Canadian Jewish Chronicle, May 1, 1931.

held in which the participants wore uniforms, replete with swastika, and gave the Fascist salute. Publications such as *Le Goglu* and *Le Patriote* told the anti-Semitic lie. We were shocked and frightened at the support which made them possible.

By the mid-thirties, this had expanded to Ottawa. In the Ottawa edition of *Le Patriote*, my father and his business became a target of attack. This excerpt from the Ottawa edition of May 16, 1935, is typical. (All excerpts from *Le Patriote* are translated from the French):

> Our forefathers did not found and colonize this country to provide the means for Freiman and a horde of Jews to enrich themselves. The British flag flies over anti-Jews as much as over Jews. Since this flag grants liberty we take advantage of this liberty to defend ourselves against the invasion of Jews.

The attack was an emotional appeal to racial, religious and economic concerns of French Canadians in the years when the Depression was still being strongly felt. As in a great deal of effective propaganda, the situation was over-simplified to "we" and "they."

In an article entitled "Christian Charity and Christians," in the Ottawa edition of June 13, 1935, the Jews were seen as aliens, even denied to be Canadians:

> Christian charity, in which we believe and which the Jew will soon learn to his detriment, requires that if there is success, prosperity, trade and commerce and thriving industries to be had by someone in Canada, that it be first for a Canadian; if there is to be supremacy, whether it be financial, industrial, commercial, professional or social, in Canada, then it must be the supremacy of Canadians; if a certain mentality, tradition, civilization or aspirations can exist in our country they must first be those of Canadians. Now, all Canadians are Christians, and the first duty of Christian charity is to protect and guarantee oneself against all which may be anti-Christian, that is to say, prejudicial to themselves. And Jews, because they are militant anti-Christians, signify a real danger for Canadians in all spheres both material and spiritual.

According to *Le Patriote* (the Ottawa edition, May 23, 1935), one of the obvious solutions to the Jewish problem in Canada was as follows:

It would be enough if Christians stopped buying from Jews and making them rich, and would buy instead from Christians. In this way, they will give Christians the financial strength necessary to support Christian charities, which are sorely in need of help, and, at the same time, will put an end to the peril of Jewish domination. Let us buy everything from Christians, never from Jews.

The paper exhorted its readers to boycott Jewish businesses and listed stores which they believed to be run or owned by Jews. The September 19 edition carried this "retraction":

Unfortunately, a correspondent of *Le Patriote* in Ottawa made an error in designating the "Star Shoe Repairing" at 3314 Dalhousie as belonging to Jews. They are not Jews, neither in race, heart or spirit. The names of the owners misled him. He had not gone to see whether the owners had hooked noses. They did not.

We awoke one morning to find a huge, black swastika painted on our front door and felt sadness at the loss of the quiet life my father valued so highly in Ottawa.

My father believed that Canadians would not tolerate such viciousness, and decided that he would fight this evil in the courtroom. So began a long and difficult legal struggle. Anti-Semitic activities were undertaken in Ottawa by Jean Tissot, a detective with the Ottawa police force. On May 29, 1935, Father launched two informations charging against Tissot for defamatory libel.

In the first information, my father charged that on May 13, 1935, Jean Tissot "did unlawfully publish a defamatory libel concerning the said A.J. Freiman to William McCullough Graham of the City of Ottawa, and Herbert Grenville Munroe, of the same place, in the form of a typewritten translation of a certain article in a newspaper known as 'Le Patriote' which said translation was headed 'Ottawa Jewry Moans,' and contains the following defamatory statements concerning the said A.J. Freiman.'' (As reported in the Ottawa *Citizen*, May 29, 1935.)

This information included excerpts of the article and their interpretation by the informant, my father, as follows:

> Meaning thereby that the said A.J. Freiman was associated with and is in sympathy with the torture and slaughter of Christians.
>
> Meaning thereby that the said A.J. Freiman is a dishonest and unethical business man and is unworthy of the trust and confidence of the public and is a loathsome and repulsive character.
>
> Meaning thereby that the said A.J. Freiman is addicted to dishonest and criminal business methods.
>
> Meaning thereby that the said A.J. Freiman is a treacherous and despicable character.

In the second information my father charged that Tissot "did unlawfully publish to William McCullough Graham, of the City of Ottawa, and Herbert Grenville Munroe, of the same place, a copy of a newspaper called 'Le Patriote,' Ottawa edition, dated May 16, 1935, which contains therein and on the front page thereof a defamatory picture or cartoon with a caption and description annexed thereto which was defamatory of the said A.J. Freiman." In this case the informant charged "that the said cartoon in connection with the caption and description means or was intended to mean that the said A.J. Freiman was a dishonest businessman, a despicable character and was unworthy of the confidence and trust of the community."

During the preliminary hearing, as reported in the Ottawa *Citizen* of Friday, June 21, 1935, Mr. Munroe, general manager of Bryson-Graham's department store in Ottawa was asked to testify. "Mr. Munroe said six months previously Mr. Tissot brought him a paper published in Chicago and attacking Jewish merchants. 'He told me the time had come for Christian merchants in Ottawa to organize to drive the Jews out of Ottawa. He told me he had used a great deal of his own finances in the work and needed financial support. He suggested that I organize a League of Christian Merchants to assist in the 'good work' and

52

also suggested it would be a good way to get rid of competition. I told him I would have nothing to do with it.'"

Defence counsel J.V. Vincent rested his argument on the legal point that libel did not apply to racial groups. He maintained that the publication of the article was an attack upon the Jews, that A.J. Freiman's name appeared not as an individual but as a man belonging to a race. Here is what Ottawa people read in the Ottawa *Evening Citizen*, June 26, 1935:

When the case was called Mr. Vincent advanced the argument that the article published did not contain a libel and that therefore there was not sufficient evidence on which to commit Tissot for trial. . .

Addressing the court Mr. Vincent declared that the publication of the article in "Le Patriote" was, first of all, an attack upon the Jews. The name of Freiman appeared in it not as an individual but as a man belonging to a race against which there was a campaign owing to their business methods and their attempt to gain control of all human activities in this as in all other countries. . .

Continuing, Mr. Vincent said the articles complained of were against the Jews and Mr. Freiman was mentioned as president of a secret society of Jews who we know are working not only in this country but in all other countries. . . .

"Mr. Freiman is a public man and as a public man is liable to be criticized in his actions," said Mr. Vincent. "There is reason for connecting him with the campaign against the Jews of which he is the head in this country. We wish to point out that there is no libel in linking Freiman with the statements concerning the Jews."

On June 28, Magistrate Glenn E. Strike ruled that there was sufficient evidence against Tissot to commit him to trial by jury at the fall assizes of the Supreme Court of Ontario.

As that trial began, we all knew that by implication my father, and Jews in general, were as much on trial as Jean Tissot. That quickly became evident in the line of questioning directed at my father, as reported in the *Citizen*, October 9:

"You are connected with the Zionist Organization in Canada?" Mr. Vincent asked.

"I am. I am president of the organization and very conversant with the Jewish movement in the whole Dominion."

"What is the purpose of the Zionist Organization?"

"We establish a home in Palestine for the Jews."

"How large is Palestine?"

"It is approximately 150 miles by 60 miles."

"Do you expect to establish all the Jews there?"

"No, not at all."

"There are other races in Palestine are there not?"

"Certainly. The Arabs form seventy per cent of the population."

Asked about the number of Jews in this country, Father stated that there were 150,000 Jewish people in Canada. In Toronto there were 30,000, in Montreal 50,000 and in Ottawa 3,000, he testified, while some 4,000,000 Jews resided in the United States.

Mr. Vincent asked, "Are all these funds you collect used in repatriation only?"

"Nothing else."

"How many Jews could you place in Palestine?"

"The Zionist movement figures on placing 5,000,000 Jews there."

Father stated that Arabs were benefiting greatly through the Jewish people in Palestine, so much so that they were coming in from other countries. "It is the only country in the world that is prosperous in these times of depression," he said.

"Is it not true that the Jewish ideal and the Christian ideal are absolutely opposite?" the defence lawyer asked.

"That is not true."

"How about the Talmud?"

"I know very little about it and few people in Ottawa know anything about it. I did when I was a child, but it is a very deep and complicated study."

"You are a great advertiser of your business, are you not?"

"I advertise like any other business man."

"When you donate to hospitals and other charities you keep your eye on the public, do you not?"

"No, I give to charities only as a citizen who desires to help them."

"Do you do business with the General Hospital?"

"I believe we have done some."

"Do you do any business with the Hull Hospital or the Salvation Army Hospital?"

"I cannot say."

"With the Civic Hospital?"

"I think we have done some business with that hospital."

These insinuations were deeply repugnant to Father because they affronted his love of people.

In his address to the jury, the defence lawyer said:

"Mr. Freiman, instead of proceeding against the root of the evil proceeded against one individual man who only gave a translation of the article to W.M. Graham and H.G. Munroe (sic), of Bryson-Graham Limited. You men, some of you are business men, know the sort of competition being carried on by merchants along Rideau, Sparks and Bank Streets. There is a hidden motive behind the prosecution of Mr. Tissot and while we have not been able to get to the bottom of it, we know it exists. Why did Mr. Freiman not sue the paper itself that was circulating the libel all over the city and province?

"You all know what is happening in business today. Was there anything very mean in Mr. Tissot asking Christians to organize to protect themselves against the Jews and to save your trade? As to the caricature contained in the paper, we see similar ones every day depicting the Prime Minister and Mr. King, yet these men do not take action against anyone. The paper only repeats the speech of A.L. Sachar, and I say there was no libel in publishing a piece that lauds Mr. Freiman."

Mr. Justice Kelly addressed the jury, defining the law in cases of criminal libel:

"Libel of the kind charged in this case is called defamatory libel, which means libel that has been published without legal justification or excuse and designed to injure or hurt the person against whom it was published. In cases of this kind the accused must justify his act on the grounds that the publication was for the public good. I brought that to the attention of counsel for the accused before this trial was proceeded with, asking whether the accused would enter a special plea. His counsel said no, that a not guilty plea would be entered as there was no libel here.

"You must decide whether the public peace has been endangered. If you find that it has, you must find the accused guilty," his Lordship concluded.

On October 9, after deliberating for two hours, the jury found Tissot guilty as charged.*

At the time of the trial, Tissot was seeking election in the federal riding of Ottawa East, emphasizing his anti-Jewish and anti-Communist attitudes. An edition of *Le Patriote*, dated October 17, urged voters to support him:

> By voting for Jean Tissot, you will show to the Jew your will to see him stand aside before the Christian, and you will make clear to communism your belief in the incontestable superiority of Christian principles to provide peace for our people. By voting for Jean Tissot, in addition to forcing back the Jewish invader, you will have given a Christian the power necessary to fight effectively for Christians, you will have given him the chance to devote all his efforts to freeing those of our own people who already feel the claws of Jewry digging into their throats.

When the election results were in, E.R.E. Chevrier had been re-elected. The legal system had supported my father, and the electorate had rejected Tissot. But we were left with a sickening feeling of loss that such deep prejudice could be found here. Incredibly, "it *did* happen here," in the city and country we loved so dearly. It is not a cliché to say that freedom must be continually earned and, if necessary, fought for.

*Father's solicitor was the late distinguished Brigadier A.W. Beament.

After the trial, watching the mounting madness in Europe, Father prophetically saw the impending war. In 1938 he feared "Democracy and freedom are being pilloried and the madness of it is that as the torturers go systematically about their nefarious business, the spectators stand by in horror-stricken amazement, with hands paralyzed and with not a voice raised in condemnation, so callous have they already become at the oft-repeated spectacle. A new generation is being schooled in a new philosophy and within the next few decades, revengeful persecution of the helpless will be accepted as calmly and as much a matter of fact as was an *auto-da-fe* five hundred years ago. And there is a further danger, for those that stand by are themselves in peril of being engulfed in the maelstrom. The mad music of the tyrant's devil-dance little by little may drag others into his inferno of hatred."

War was declared in September of 1939.

In the agony of global war, many priorities are re-ordered. All of us knew that unless the Nazi machine was destroyed, there could be no Jewish state. As 1943 drew to a close, it appeared that victory for the Allies was in sight, and the struggle for Jewish statehood could be rejoined with vigour.

On December 3 that year, Father wrote this letter to Prime Minister Mackenzie King:

My Dear Mr. Prime Minister:

Sometime ago you were good enough to say that you would keep very much in mind certain thoughts which I had previously expressed on behalf of the Jewish people. I am now taking advantage of your kindness to approach you on the question of Palestine. In doing so I am acting, not only in my personal capacity, but as the head and on behalf of the Zionist movement in Canada which, as you have no doubt had reason to observe, has the active support of all sections and classes of Jewry in this country, as well as the sympathy of numerous influential leaders and groups among non-Jewish Canadians.

From the contacts and conversations I have had with you on this subject, I know that there is no need to state the problem here, nor to review in detail the historical and political developments since the time when the Balfour Declaration of 1917, which was subsequently incorporated into the British Mandate for Palestine in 1922, committed Great Britain, with the concurrence of the League of Nations, including Canada, and the United States, to the establishment in Palestine of a national home for the Jewish people. You are familiar, I know, with the humanitarian reasons which prompted the Declaration, with the fact that it has been reiterated by every British government since that time, and with the great achievements wrought in that tiny neglected country by harried and homeless Jews from Europe whose numbers now exceed half a million, and with the consequent benefits enjoyed by Palestine's whole population, Christian, Arab and Jew alike.

If a Jewish homeland in Palestine was necessary twenty-six years ago and if it has more than justified its existence in the intervening years, its need now and in the years following this war, will be so much greater, when literally millions of Jews who can never return to live in the midst of peoples whose minds will be poisoned with Nazi doctrines for generations to come, must needs find a home where their human right to work and live by the fruits of their work will be assured. Is it not therefore appalling to contemplate that this opportunity will be denied them by the stoppage of future Jewish immigration into Palestine after March, 1944? And yet that will be the inevitable result if a British White Paper of May, 1939, is to be enforced.

The White Paper, you will remember, promulgated in an hour of Britain's weakness, was denounced in Parliament, at the time by Mr. Amery, Mr. Morrison, the Archbishop of Canterbury and many others, including Mr. Churchill, by whom it was characterized as "a plain breach of a solemn obligation...the destruction of the Balfour Declaration..." and "A one-sided denunciation of an engagement." That White Paper was accepted by the British House of Commons only because the government insisted on making it a vote of confidence, and because the period was one of grave international complications. One month later, although presented personally by Mr. Malcolm MacDonald, then Colonial Secretary, it was formally disapproved of by the Permanent Mandates Commission and was never submitted to the Council of the League of Nations.

As the date for carrying this new policy into effect draws near, a great surge of public feeling throughout the English-speaking world is making itself felt. Jewish masses everywhere, as well as non-Jewish editors, religious, labour and other groups and leaders of thought and action throughout England, the United States and Canada, including the Prime Ministers of South Africa and New Zealand, have raised their voices to urge the abolition of the policy enunciated in the White Paper and the full implementation of the Balfour Declaration, permitting free and unrestricted Jewish immigration and the maximum economic development of Palestine.

My purpose in writing to you is respectfully to suggest that the Canadian Government is not without responsibility in this matter and could, quite properly, in view of Canadian public opinion and Canada's membership in the League of Nations, make appropriate representations to the British Government along the lines indicated above. It was originally suggested to me that a delegation be selected and that a request be submitted for an audience at which these views might be presented to you. I have, however, thought it better to place the situation before you in this way in the hope that you will be able to consider it and advise me as to the steps you are able to take. Needless to say, I shall be in readiness at any time to discuss the question with you in person and to provide you with any further information you may require.

Sincerely yours,
A.J. Freiman

The reply from the Prime Minister, whom Father valued as a friend, was an exercise typical of Mr. King. It was couched in pseudo-diplomatic, tedious, illogical language.

My dear Mr. Freiman,

Absence from Ottawa has prevented me from acknowledging sooner your letter of December 3, in which you suggest that the Canadian Government, in view of this country's membership in the League of Nations, might properly make representations to the United Kingdom Government for withdrawal of the White Paper of 1939.

Canada has a direct interest in the settlement of the Jewish problem on a basis which will provide permanent security for the Jewish people. None of us can forget that the precariousness of the Jewish position was one of the circumstances contributing to the rise to power of the enemy. Thus membership in the United Nations as well as League membership lays on this country responsibility for giving attention to the position of the Jews with a view to the achievement of genuine security by the Jewish people in the post-war era.

Whether the specific proposal you suggest would be the best contribution the Canadian Government could make is a matter on which, I understand, there is some difference of opinion among Jews as well as non-Jews. I believe the policy of the White Paper was directed not toward closing the doors of Palestine against further Jewish immigration but toward creating political conditions which would facilitate peaceful development of the Jewish National Home. It proposes the fulfilment of certain guarantees embodied in the Covenant and the mandate which have been held in abeyance during the period in which the Jewish National Home has been given its start, in the belief that without these guarantees the Jewish National Home cannot enjoy in the future the security its friends all desire for it, which the mandate was intended to assure it.

To ask for withdrawal of the White Paper now would be to condemn in advance the effort to establish democratic procedures and the principle that both elements of the Palestinian population must be consulted about policies which closely affect their interests. In present conditions in the Near East, there is a very real danger that a failure to settle the problem of immigration by agreement would result in an appeal to force involving not only Palestine but also neighbouring territories.

It is certainly not for lack of interest in remedying the intolerable position of the Jews in Europe today that the Canadian Government has not acted long since in the sense suggested in your letter–namely, to press for withdrawal of the White Paper and for promotion of a larger immigration into Palestine than was contemplated in the British undertakings to the Jews as defined in the Churchill White Paper of 1922. Due weight has had to be given to the view that the most urgent requirement is to secure conditions of stability both in Palestine and in Europe, which will enable individual Jews to make their own free choice as to where they shall live. Canada's participation in the war is the best contribution it can make toward rendering mass emigrations from Europe unnecessary. The creation of conditions in Palestine which will assure the steady development of the Jewish National Home is a matter which can hardly be effected except by agreement among those whose interests are directly concerned.

It may be true as you suggest that such agreement cannot be reached immediately. There is reason to hope, however, that it will become possible when the pressure of persecution has been removed from the lives of European Jews and the pressure of fear from the minds of the Arabs. The victory of the United Nations will remove the first pressure, which will immediately affect the second and thereby enable moderate Arab and Jewish leaders to arrive at an understanding such as is still unfortunately lacking.

That exchange of letters was a vivid reflection of the years and years of frustration that Father, and Zionists throughout the world, encountered in their untiring quest for Jewish statehood.

Father did not live to see the dream fulfilled. He died on June 4, 1944, nearly three and a half years before Israel was proclaimed as a Jewish state on November 29, 1947.

It was the store, of course, that made possible the many other mansions of my father's house.

Of all his interests, the store was the most consuming, and Father was happiest when he was "on the floor," greeting customers, making certain that they were being well served.

The Archibald J. Freiman Department Store at 73 Rideau, later to be A.J. Freiman Ltd., had a thirty-foot red brick front and was one hundred feet deep. Its three storeys were supported by old logs holding up the street floor and a dugout area below of about three feet. My first memories are of large tables of women's blouses and lingerie. At the back of the store was a place for people to pay their accounts, and two offices. One was Father's, the other was occupied by a Mr. Peabody, who assumed a myth-like quality for me for two reasons. First, I hardly ever saw him; second, he sounded mysteriously independent because he was a "freelance" advertising man. The intriguing thing about his office were the copper engravings. One could place a paper on top of an engraving and by rubbing quite hard could produce a marvellous upside-down picture.

I remember Father saying one day, "What a great ad Peabody wrote." It was a picture of the ocean with giant waves. The caption underneath said, "What are the wild waves saying, Nellie? Freiman's of course." I guess the ad must have worked.

On the second floor were dresses and coats. On the third were draperies, toys, carpets, and other furnishings. On this floor came my first job at the age of ten–salesman in the toy department during Christmas holidays. I was excited and pleased about my "grown-up" job until I heard of something called "internal audit." This was a mysterious group who could instantly find the most minute mistake on a sales bill. My arithmetic left much to be desired, and I lived in constant fear that the "boss's son" would make a horrendous error and be found out by the internal audit. Despite this, and a few other fears, my early sales career went rather well. I loved the busy nights and the occasional customer who expressed appreciation at my politeness or for serving well.

Even in those youthful days, I was aware that Father kept buying and acquiring more properties and becoming ever busier. Yet, on Sundays he would repair to the living room or sometimes the conservatory to read. His library was precious to him, and despite his business, his organizational activities, and his family, he somehow found time to satisfy his voracious appetite for reading. It is not surprising that despite his late start in English education he became a man of letters whose writings and addresses reflected a rare knowledge of and ability to use the language to its beautiful advantage.

But Father did not have the luxury of reading every Sunday.

On "working Sundays" he would take me with him by train to Montreal, leaving before 8:00 A.M. in order to arrive by 11:00. On those white, cold winter days, a horse and sleigh met us at the old CNR Bonaventure Station. From there we would proceed to the first dress or coat manufacturer who, through kindness, or because Dad "bought big," opened his doors on Sundays as a special favour. The long racks of dresses and coats fascinated me. Dad walked along them quickly, feeling the fabric and pulling every fourth or fifth garment out to look at the style. He would then ask, simply: "How many have you got?" The man would say how many he had, 400 perhaps. Dad would ask, "How much do you want?" Whatever the price, there was always a counter offer. If the bargaining became serious and there was a dollar or fifty-cent difference, Dad would inevitably say: "I'll flip you for it." He would produce a quarter, flip it, feel the "tails" side, and turn the coin with that side up. He usually won because his opponents were inclined to say, "Heads." Dad always enjoyed being able to create such a psychological advantage. He must have lost sometimes, but we never heard about it. After a deal was made, happy words were exchanged, and we would head off in the sleigh to the next manufacturer. There was no time to be lost. We always had a number of stops, and we had to catch the 4:00 train so that Dad could get me home at a time satisfactory to Mother. Any time after 7:00 was very late. Those Sundays were elixir and balm to the small spirit and allowed me to enter the big business world, and to ride on a train. Tea on the train included CNR muffins and thick, well-browned, toast and tons of marmalade and jam. What Sundays they were!

Over the years, more departments were added to the store, including the men's department on the main floor, where I was to work two very dull summers. I remember more hoardings and more building until Freiman's reached the corner. Now it was a big store—three storeys, 200' x 200'. All the old red brick fronts of the original building were as they had been. To expand was to pull the walls down, put in whatever steel was required, bring in tables and racks and inexpensive fixtures, and sell more goods. It sounds easy, but I know that it wasn't. Dad worked hard, and found great satisfaction in his accomplishments. Then came a white stone facing for the front and, in 1929, the great expansion – two more storeys and a new stone facing on the side of the building.

The two additional storeys enabled Father to achieve his long-held goal of a full-line department store – including a complete furniture department. And therein was spawned a problem. Some of Ottawa's larger furniture dealers, knowing of Father's competitive ability that allowed him to underprice most other stores, informed the key Canadian furniture manufacturers that if they supplied Freiman's, the old customers would stop buying. The manufacturers got the message and refused to sell to my father. With his usual knack for turning a problem into an opportunity, Father went to Grand Rapids, Michigan, where he bought several carloads of top quality furniture at an attractive, high-volume price. Bringing it back to Ottawa, he priced it to sell at very little over his cost, thus beating his competitors' prices throughout the entire Ottawa area, and beyond. The Canadian manufacturers got that message, too, and Father was invited to buy whatever furniture they wished to sell. That marked the start of a long and happy relationship between Freiman's and the Canadian furniture industry.

In all business matters, Father had a sixth sense, an intuitive know-how. To "buy big," even when the store was small, was imperative. His first big buy was from Ben Gardner, who later married Edgar Berliner's wife and took over the Berliner Company RCA Victor. In these early days Mr. Gardner had operated a large men's clothing factory and was stuck with 5,000 men's suits. Dad bought them all for $5 each. He marked them according to quality in three groups – $10, $15, and $20 – meeting his three essential prerequisites: the suits were of good quality, customers received a real value, and the venture was profitable.

From the beginning Dad was a "big buyer." Two thousand dresses were bought in the old Jacobs building in minutes after a last flip for 50 cents a dress. Dad won, so the cost difference was $1,000. He loved the excitement of buying, of advertising, and of the crowds that flocked to buy his large purchases. And the crowds did come, and the business prospered.

In the summer of 1921, Dad was off to Europe with Mother for a month's holiday. He returned to a seemingly difficult situation. The recession of 1921 was serious, business was extremely slow, and inventories everywhere were high. But manufacturers were also overstocked and anxious to sell, so Dad courageously went out for "big buys" to add to his overstocked inventories. There were bargains everywhere. He bought them and then worked out a strategy to sell them, and thus began the tradition of Freiman's Birthday Sales. The focal point was a gigantic birthday cake weighing over a ton. In the large corner window was an artistic city built of coins. With each purchase, customers could fill in a slip estimating the number of coins. The closest estimates won tremendous prizes. The first, second, and third prizes were automobiles, and there were many other lesser prizes. A potential business reversal was converted into a great success.

These were productive, happy days for Father. He was just over forty years old, he had a well-established business, he was a civic and national leader, with Mother establishing her own wide reputation, and he had his homes. He would often say to his children, with his great laugh and that sparkle in his eyes, "Yes, and even my children aren't so bad."

In business, as in all other things, Father's standards were as high as his temper when his standards weren't met. For Father, there were no shades to the word "honest." A statement was either honest or it was dishonest. He demanded that his advertisements bend backwards in this respect. This principle was so well engrained that Freiman's became a difficult employer for many buyers, merchandise managers, and sales promotion managers. Each advertisement was a personal responsibility—a trust entered into between my father and the customer.

Dad's criteria for service were equally high. One Christmas season, soon after I had joined the store full time, I was invited to a "Deb" ball at the golf club. (In those days debutantes were "presented" at rather sumptuous, white-tie parties.) It was around 3:30 A.M. Christmas Eve when I returned home—to a ringing telephone. I was informed by a very annoyed gentleman that the toys he had bought for his children had not been delivered. I took his name and address and gave him my word that I would deliver the toys myself first thing in the morning.

About 9:00 A.M. I looked in on Mother and Dad on my way to the store. I told Dad about the toys and was shocked when he became extremely angry with me. "But this is Christmas morning, and those children do not have their toys." In a "spoken from the heart" moment I was told I should have gone to the store immediately when I received the call. He was not asking me to do anything he had not done himself.

A few years earlier, when a pair of skis had not been delivered by 4:00 A.M. Christmas morning, Dad went to the store, called the sporting goods buyer, and someone to attach the fittings, and personally delivered the parcel to the customer's home. But his efforts were not appreciated. Having not thought to ask the make of the skis, he took the most expensive ones in the store. That morning at 10:00 the customer telephoned to inform Father that the skis he had delivered were not the right ones. Father explained that these were better skis and that, of course, there would be no extra charge. Father also told him of what had happened between 4:00 A.M. and 7:00 A.M. and how the skis were delivered. When the man became rude, I heard Father speaking without temper, but in cold, even terms.

"Mr. —, I have tried to satisfy you, but I have not succeeded. You do not appreciate what I have tried to do. In the future you will please take your business somewhere else. If I ever see you in our store again, I will personally have you physically removed. Goodbye."

One of Father's basic principles was his belief in the honesty of people. He established, soon after opening the store, what was then called "an installment house" at Freiman's. Customers could pay for purchases over a period of time by installments. There was no charge for credit but a substantial 20-per-cent penalty levied if accounts were not paid on time.

As a merchant, Father had the keenest perception. He would watch the face of a customer to see reactions to merchandise, the sales person's manner of selling, and appearance. He could see a speck of dust at twelve feet. Often, on leaving the store and driving slowly past it, he would see something wrong in a display window–a card that was crooked, a thread hanging from the seam of a dress, or an unharmonious colour. He would immediately return to the store, summon the responsible personnel, correct the problem, smile with satisfaction, and start again for home.

The 1929 expansion had added 84,000 square feet of

space – and fulfilled Father's earlier promise to the bank president. Freiman's was now the largest department store in Ottawa, both in sales and in size. As restlessly energetic as ever and caught up, like everyone else, in the boom-times mood of the late twenties, Father decided to open two new small department stores, one near Ottawa at Renfrew, and a hundred miles away at Pembroke. It was a logical time to expand. Everyone was happy because money was everywhere, and the stock market was booming. With a 10 per cent down payment and the rest on margin you owned stock on the big board – and all stocks were going up.

The late twenties was a time of joy transcended only by frenzy; a maniacal time of activity and excitement given voice in the Charleston, the speakeasy, the short-fringed flapper dresses, the too-flashy cars, the big talkie movies, and exaggerated bigness and gaucherie everywhere. Then came October 1929. The New York stock market crashed on a Thursday, and was followed by the *coup de grâce* of the following Tuesday. Father, too, had been caught in the excitement of winning on the market in those heady days. On that grim Thursday he lost a large sum of money and sold all his market holdings before the horrendous, following Tuesday.

Despite the economic chaos in most of the rest of the world, business continued satisfactorily in Ottawa until early 1931. The Liberal government of Mackenzie King had lost the election of 1930 to R.B. Bennett. Mr. Bennett delivered an economic blow to Ottawa by cutting public service salaries by 10 per cent and by closing certain departments of government. All public servants were affected, and business in Ottawa quickly felt the impact.

These were fateful days for my father as shades of darkness appeared everywhere. To finance the expansion in 1929, he had issued a preferred stock, which had voting rights that could be activated if dividends were not paid. As business grew worse, it was necessary to discontinue dividends, and the preferred shareholders could then have voting control. But they showed complete confidence in Dad, and were certain that he could solve the problem. He considered the sale of the business but found that it could not be sold because of a 30' x 100' section in the centre of the building that was not owned by the company, but leased. For many years, the owner had refused to sell—and refused again now. Obviously, this made the business unsaleable at any reasonable price. It was years later before I succeeded in making the purchase.

The strain on Father was made more difficult by Mother's continuing illness and the advancing madness in Nazi Germany.

Such were the circumstances when I decided to leave Harvard Business School, after one year, and join the business to help in whatever way I could. I had done well enough at McGill to be admitted to the Harvard Graduate School of Business Administration, and had entered "The Factory" in September 1931. I was assigned a room in Mellon Hall dorm and presented myself for the opening lecture. Dean Donham, no doubt a fine academician, but humourless and rather frightening, began by apprising his crop of freshmen of two facts: tests would be given within six weeks and anyone who was not, in the view of the faculty, "making it" would be asked to leave. Second, if anyone felt overworked or suffering from nervous stress, he was to report to the Harvard Business School doctor at an address on Brattle Street in Cambridge. The Dean felt that the nervous breakdowns and the one suicide of the previous term could have been avoided had those students sought medical advice sooner. With that introduction began the slow, unceasing work on subjects, most of which I found extremely boring, and all of which were presented in virtually incomprehensible business jargon.

The main relief from the drudgery was my new Ford convertible, a high-spirited beauty, maroon with yellow wire wheels, a spare on the left front fender, and the gas-tank cap right in front of the windshield—all for $486, complete with licence. That car, the drive to the all-girl Wellesley College for a date, back to Boston for dancing at the Copley-Plaza or Ritz Hotel, and back to Wellesley in time for the girls' 1:00 A.M. curfew gave us brief but pleasurable breaks from the slavery of school.

But these trips were really just tune-ups for the major escapes—the 1:00 P.M. Saturday train to New York would get us there in plenty of time to clean up before hitting the speakeasies on 52nd Street. We would start near the corner and sit at the bar to hear Wingy Minone, the talented one-armed trumpet player. Pat Harrington would hold forth at Leon and Eddies'; we would talk at Angelo's and meet new and old friends at the bar. Once we were regaled by the master of them all, Robert Benchley, quite the most entertaining conversationalist in New York, who had made a short film, *The Sex Life of the Polyp*, and was writing superb, small pieces for the *New Yorker*. Across the street, Billie Holiday was singing her bitterest and saddest song of all – the first real cry of horror at black injustice that I had ever heard. The song was "Strange Fruit," a bitter tale of a black body gently swaying from a tree in the wind, having been lynched. Then on to Red Norvo, playing xylophone with his famous trio, and eventually to Harlem; Small's Paradise with the tap-dancing waiters or Barron's Exclusive – great entertainment in a smoky, dingy cellar – or maybe to see Cab Calloway in his white tails at the Cotton Club. Then Sunday, exhausted but refreshed, we went back to the grind in Boston.

Quite some time before the spring exams I had concluded that Harvard and I would each benefit more apart than together. Father had reluctantly accepted my decision and while I agreed to complete the term and write exams, I did precious little to prepare for them. That did not concern me particularly because I had always been an easy learner and had completed undergraduate school with very satisfactory grades. But the Harvard results were mortifying. I flunked two of the courses, a personal embarrassment not offset by having passed all the others and earning a distinction of over 95 per cent in one of them.

And so, after the rarified atmosphere of Harvard and Boston, New York and Harlem, I returned to Ottawa and Freiman's in June of 1931. I was twenty-two years of age, an immediate vice-president, and entering the department store business at the lowest depths of the Depression. On my first morning at the store, Father said simply, "Son there is so much to do. I have not the time to train you in anything. You will have to find out for yourself. Get to work – and good luck!"

However necessary that rather brusque welcome was, it did nothing to increase my low level of real interest and sense of involvement. I had not really wanted to come back to Ottawa and go into the store, but felt compelled to do so because of the situation facing Mother and Father. I had grown steadily further apart from Father as our paths and interests had diverged in recent years. My real interests in those days were girls and cars, theatre and good food, attractive people, and the new talking motion pictures. I could see myself going to Hollywood and combining my new business training with my compelling dream to produce and direct a movie. But as it happens with so many of our dreams, the more practical realities take precedence. Naturally, I returned to confirmations of orders and accounting procedures, etc., but, because the decision to come home had been solely mine, it was something I never regretted.

For at least the first ten months I was devastated most of the time, simply because I did not know where or how "to go to work." The harder I tried, the worse I did. My "bright, new" ideas just would not work, and usually they cost money. I received my first real lesson in money that summer.

Father had been summoned to the head office of the bank in Toronto and asked me to go with him. The visit was unpleasant and unforgettable for the hypocrisy and cold, good manners that were displayed. We entered the waiting-room of the executive offices of the Canadian Bank of Commerce, and were seated in hard-backed oak, fake *petit-point* chairs. Looking down from their positions on the walls of that vast hexagonal room were all the former chairmen of the bank, peering at us with cold, stern eyes from their great canvasses, surrounded by large, overly ornate gold frames. After a few moments, we were guided to the office of the great man. There, after the dull amenities had been observed, and after being assured of the total confidence that the bank placed in my father's personal ability and in the business, we were told that "for our protection" the bank had decided to cut our line of credit by a substantial amount. Father pointed out that this would mean our already low inventories would have to be cut further, with resulting losses. The only reply was that the credit line had to be cut. It was one of the very few times that I had seen Father crushed and subdued. We returned to Ottawa and went about cutting our inventories and taking the losses. We cut staff and reduced salaries, all of which was crippling to everyone's morale. It was a basic fight for survival. My only advantage was that I was young at a time when the strain was aging Dad too quickly.

In those difficult days, just to get people inside the store, it was necessary to try every kind, or any kind, of promotion – including Sally Rand. Sally had been the hit of the 1933 Chicago World's Fair when she stripped behind those huge pink feather fans. She was coming to Ottawa and when she arrived I convinced her to do a fashion show at Freiman's with her line of girls performing as models. I told her that the publicity would be sensational. For once I was right – more right than I had counted on. The night of the show the crowds wanting to see Sally were so great that we could not get enough police protection, and women were pushed through the front display windows by the sheer weight of people crowding to get in. Fortunately no one was seriously hurt but a Canadian press story was carried in newspapers across the country. My father had been in New York and was returning by train via Montreal when he saw the story. It was date-lined Ottawa and no department store name was given. But he knew it was his son "at work." The next day the store was almost empty again. The gloom continued.

One momentous event brightened my personal life early in 1934. Father had decided to send my younger sister Queene and me on a tour to Palestine, arranged by Mother's close colleague in Hadassah, Rose Dunkelman of Toronto. Looking back, Dad did not think that I was interested enough in Palestine. He believed my outside interests were frivolous. In any event, we embarked early in February on the *S.S. Manhattan* for Cherbourg and then to Paris. The first person I met was Audrey Steinkopf. Travelling with Mrs. Dunkelman, she was from Winnipeg and was attending Ontario Ladies' College, a private girls' school near Toronto. The Dunkelmans had practically adopted her. I knew that my family knew her family from Winnipeg, where her father, Max Steinkopf, K.C., was a distinguished lawyer.

It was not long before Queene and I adopted Audrey. We travelled from Cherbourg to Paris to Marseilles where we boarded a small French ship, the *Marietta Pasha*. It had few passengers, a bartender with a terrific rash on his hands, which ruled out the bar for the six-day passage, and three small dining rooms: one for Moslems, one kosher, and one for folks like us. The food must have been equally bad in each. Audrey complained that her cabin was impossible, a small box of a thing. I went to the captain, who was also the purser, and explained the problem. I asked if there was a cabin available near my sister. Being French, the captain had more romantic ideas. He had my sister's luggage put all the way down near the hold where Audrey's had been and Audrey's sent up to Queene's fine cabin. When I protested, he became annoyed not only at my stupidity and poor French, but also at my ineptitude in not taking advantage of the beautifully romantic situation that he had so graciously arranged.

Eventually reaching Cairo, we checked into the Semiramis Hotel. A few days later I went down to the dining room to meet Audrey for a farewell breakfast before she sailed from Alexandria. After she left, I went to Queene's room to tell her that we had been stupid in permitting her to leave without us since we (meaning me) had been having such a good time. Queene suggested that I go to Alexandria and get Audrey off the boat. I dashed down to the concierge and informed him that I had to be at the dock in Alexandria before noon that day. He said:

"*Mais, ce n'est pas possible.*"

There were no trains, planes, or anything that could "get me to the ship on time." I asked him to charter a plane for me. He did, and I raced off to Egyptian Airlines where a small two-seater Piper Cub was waiting, engine warm and ready. I jumped in and ducked my head as the plastic bubble was pulled over us. The pilot revved up and we were off. When we reached our altitude over Cairo, the pilot turned around and asked:

"For chrissake, Laurie, what are you doing here?" It was Tony Spooner who had been instructor at the McGill Light Airplane Club and who had come to Egypt to be chief pilot for Egyptian Airlines. I told him I had to get a girl off a boat in Alexandria before 12:00.

He yelled back, "Are you going to marry her?"

"Quite honestly, I really haven't thought of it," I replied, "but if she will have me, I guess I will." At least, I decided, I would ask her.

Arriving at the dock, we pushed through the mob of people hawking necklaces, small sheep, charm bracelets, aphrodisiacs, and everything else imaginable before the boat sailed. When we reached the ship's side, I spotted Audrey at the rail and yelled up to her. "You must get off the ship immediately."

"Why?" she asked.

"Let's get married this afternoon."

"I'll be right down," she said and calmly had her luggage removed, walking down the gangplank just before it was lifted and taken away. We then found, of course, that residency regulations in Egypt meant no wedding that day. Tony had by now scouted up some warm champagne and we toasted each other in the taxi on the way to the airport. Then, with Audrey on my knee in the rear seat, and Tony in rare good humour in the cockpit, we returned to Cairo to tell Queene.

Then on to Palestine where our dear friends Dr. Dov Joseph* and his wife Goldie gave an engagement party for us at their home in Jerusalem. From there we sailed to New York on the Italian liner, *The Roma*, which later sunk in the Second World War. We arrived on Wednesday and invited our families to the hotel Sherry for the wedding Sunday. We engaged Rabbi Elias Solomon, a wise and good man, and the wedding was a smashing success – with everyone except Audrey and me weeping copiously. It was March 25, 1934.

Despite my elation, and the wonder of life with Audrey, the Depression was still on. If anything, it was more difficult than ever because everyone knew now that it would not end quickly.

I worked hard to establish a rapport with my associates and to overcome the dual stigma of being "the boss's son" and a "Harvard Business School genius." I opened the store every morning at 7:40 and was usually the last to leave. Life then was one sales promotion after another: a $1-day on Wednesday, followed by an eighty-eight-cent day on Thursday, and "Freiman Day" the next week.

One of my jobs was to supervise the two small stores Dad had opened in Renfrew and Pembroke in 1929 as trial stores for a chain of department stores in small cities. I would take the 7:50 A.M. train, with its wood-fired, pot-bellied stove in the passenger coach. We would arrive at Renfrew at 10:20, and in mid-winter, with the few mills of the town closed, one could look down the

*Dr. Dov Joseph was a distinguished lawyer, originally from Montreal, who settled in Palestine in 1921. He served as Military Governor of Jerusalem during the 1947 War of Independence, and held no fewer than seven Cabinet posts during his years as a minister of the Israeli government.

main street and see nary a soul. I was usually the lone customer for lunch at the Hotel Renfrew, which was immaculate in those debt-ridden days, and served good food with the ease and charm of a truly good restaurant.

Work in Renfrew lasted until the train left at 6:15 P.M. for arrival in Pembroke an hour later. Then dinner and work and the 1:30 train home, arriving in Ottawa at 4:30 A.M. Fortunately, passengers were allowed to sleep until a decent hour, because the trains were kept in the yards for some time. That was a weekly routine for many months, and I learned a lot from those small stores.

I was married, working hard and, I felt, getting nowhere. At first Audrey and I had an apartment in the posh apartment-hotel of those days, the Roxborough. The following year we rented a small furnished bungalow for $85 a month. But after cutting my salary to $50 a week, as business grew tighter, I proposed that we move into my father's large house in order to save money. My Mother objected because she did not feel it was fair to Audrey, but we really had no other choice.

Often during those difficult times, I would reassure myself by thinking about the way Dad had built the business. I recalled his description of the difficulties he had in getting started, the first store, and then the store at 73 Rideau. I remembered the "working Sunday" trips with him to Montreal, when he would flip a coin to settle the bargaining over a price. And I thought often about driving with him to see his father just before grandfather's death.

Father liked especially to drive in the autumn when the leaves were changing colour. One day he asked me to go with him to Hamilton where his father was recuperating from a stroke. We arrived to find Grandfather Freiman on his balcony. He was pleased to see us, and ordered tea and cakes to be served while we chatted. The stroke had left him paralyzed on one side, but he could stand erect and was still very handsome. A patrician figure, dour and stern as ever, he asked my father, "Son, how is your son doing in the business?" Dad told him, jokingly, "Unlike your son, Dad, my son is doing just fine." My grandfather replied very seriously, "That is not so. You had to do well because I taught you everything you know!" It was the last time the three of us were together. Grandfather died later that year, after eighty-four years of a quiet, dignified life.

Working our way out of the Depression was a slow, often frustrating, process. But it had its gratifying aspects too. As we worked to solve the problems, as we enjoyed the infrequent, minor successes and triumphs, the old feelings of closeness and shared interests came back. Father and I both developed new levels of warmth and respect for each other and found a deep sense of real partnership that few fathers and sons share in later life. It was not all smiles and honey, of course; some moments of conflict are unavoidable in any strong partnership.

Many changes needed to be made to make the store work, and Father was reluctant at this point to accept change. But gradually he did. The most significant one was to charge for credit on a monthly basis, discontinuing the "free credit" and penalty for default. That change was necessary because customers who owed the penalty did not pay it and simply shopped somewhere else. There was a need for new merchandise controls, basic stock and unit controls, and more effective expense controls and systems. And much of the building was sorely in need of physical redevelopment but that could be achieved only as small amounts of money became available. It was a long, tortuous struggle, but as the "Dirty Thirties" drew to a close, it looked as though the economy generally had "turned the corner."

Then came September 1939. Germany invaded Poland on the first. England declared war on September 3. In the Canadian Parliament the vote was taken on September 9. The next day the King, on behalf of Canada, declared war against Germany.

Even though many had seen it coming, the fact that this peaceful country was formally at war was a chilling thought. There was no real question in my mind about what course of action I would take. With Audrey's unhesitating, if reluctant, support, and Mother's immediate understanding, despite her serious illness, I told Father that I would enlist for active service. He agreed. Some weeks later while I was organizing things at the store to make my absence as little felt as possible, Father was stricken with a crippling coronary thrombosis. Hours after being rushed to hospital, he suffered another. Any thought of immediate enlistment was impossible. In the tense days that followed, until we knew that Father would survive, the fact of war–and even the business–seemed remote and somehow unreal. Mostly I felt frightened, frightened for Father's life and unprepared for the responsibility that awaited me. After Father's condition had stabilized, and he had begun the long struggle to recovery, I talked at length with his doctor. His orders to me were that I should talk to Dad about the business, but never about any part of it that might cause him to worry or become upset. How simple that sounded, and how difficult it was to practise.

As his strength slowly returned, Father was permitted to come to the store occasionally for short periods if he felt up to it. On one such day, events produced the worst possible scenario for someone recuperating from a heart attack. In the afternoon I was walking slowly with him through the store when we smelled smoke. Showing more calm than I felt, I seated Father in a comfortable chair, called the store superintendent, and discovered that smoke was pouring from the roof of the store. The Fire Department had been called and arrived to find part of the roof burning. The fire chief, checking to see if the fire had spread to the middle of the roof, was greeted by great fangs of flame shooting up into the air. Another alarm was put in, and in minutes we had a four-alarm-fire on our hands. Fortunately, the blaze was confined to the roof and the chief assured me that there was no real danger to anyone in the rest of the building. I moved quickly through the store telling our people to stay calm and keep serving customers. Everyone, clerks and customers alike, behaved beautifully and by 6:00 P.M. the fire was extinguished. Dad bore all the excitement with a philosophical serenity and eventually went home, after telling me that I had done a good job.

By 8:00 the next morning, thanks to the heroic efforts of Superintendent George Joiner and his volunteers, the entire store had been cleaned up. With the whole place shining by 9:00 A.M., we opened as usual for business.

Through the spring and summer of 1940, Father gradually regained his strength and flashes of his old spirit appeared more frequently. Then, in November, Mother died. With this, Father had lost too much. His zest for living was gone, no matter how we tried to revive it.

He found some solace in turning his attention to the spiritual needs of Ottawa's Jewish community. He had been active in such matters for many years, having served as building chairman for the synagogue that was built in 1903; he had been only twenty-three. The community was now too large for that building, and Father believed that there could be Jewish fulfillment for the people in the community only through building a House of Learning (Bet Hamidrash), a House of Prayer (Bet Hatfilah), and a House of Assembly (Bet Haknesset) in one large complex. He was instrumental in forming the first committee to plan and finance the complex and was the Honorary Chairman of the Synagogue and Jewish Community Centre Committee for the first fund-raising campaign in 1943.

June 4, 1944. Father had agreed to give the eulogy and unveil a tablet in memory of Rev. Jacob Mirsky, the same reverend gentleman my grandfather, Moses Bilsky, had brought from New York many years before, sitting up with him in the train from New York, taking turns holding the scrolls of the Torah. Father had been very close to the old gentleman and he knew so well Mother's deep affection and respect for him. Keenly aware of his failing health, I pleaded with Dad frequently during the previous week not to give the eulogy. He dismissed me as a fretful busybody. On Sunday, the community assembled to pay its tribute to a noble man of the Lord who had "walked humbly before him." It was a simple service. Father sat surrounded by his family and his friends. At the appropriate moment, he walked up the stairs to the Holy Ark, paused briefly, and gave a short, moving tribute in honour of the departed clergyman. He then unveiled the tablet and quietly walked down the stairs to his seat beside me. He looked up at the stained glass window installed in honour of Mother with the inscription from King Solomon's Book of Proverbs: "Many daughters have done worthy, but thou excellest them all." He sighed deeply, and I placed my arm around his shoulders to comfort him. The choir began the ancient memorial chant "E-L Moleh Rachamim":

O Lord, who art full of compassion, who dwells on high–God of forgiveness, who art merciful, slow to anger and abounding in loving kindness, grant pardon to transgression, nearness of salvation, and perfect rest beneath the shadow of Thy divine presence in the exalted places among the holy and pure who shine as the brightness of the firmament—who has gone to his eternal home. We beseech thee, O Lord of compassion, grant unto him for good all the meritorious and pious deeds which he wrought while on earth. Open unto him the gates of righteousness and light, the gates of pity and grace. O shelter him forever under the cover of Thy wings and let his soul be bound up in the bond of eternal life. The Lord is his inheritance; may he rest in peace. And let us say, Amen.

The last verse had been sung. Father had died in my arms. The congregants wept softly as they filed out quietly. My family and I were left to mourn in the synagogue Father had helped build. For twenty-five years he had been its President, guiding the affairs of another of his houses.

June 6—the day of Father's funeral—would have been his sixty-fourth birthday. Prime Minister King delayed the announcement of the D-Day landings in order to attend the funeral. The Governor General was represented by His Excellency's Senior Secretary, Colonel H. Willis O'Connor, my father's good friend, who led the cortège of thousands following Father's casket.

A noble man had left his family and his community a proud heritage.

Chapter V

Continuing the House of Freiman

A few days after Father's dramatic death in the synagogue, I called a family meeting. My sister Dorothy lived in Ottawa with her husband Bernard, who had just left the RCAF with the rank of wing commander and returned to Ottawa to establish his legal practice. Queene came from Toronto where her husband Benjamin Luxenberg was now a well-established and successful lawyer. Father had left each of his children one-third of the company, with the provision that I would vote the family shares. The company was doing better, but I wanted my sisters and their husbands to recognize that we all faced a new period in our lives – that the house of Freiman was now without Father's guiding hand, and that my approach and style would not necessarily be the same as Father's had been. Bernard agreed to act as counsel and treasurer and Benjamin accepted the post of secretary of the company. I suppose that my feelings then were not much different than Father's had been after he bought out his father and became master of his own business. The main difference was that I was not alone, but had the legacy of Father's experience and the support of the family.

And like Father in his era, I, too, was building my other houses. As Mother had provided one of the central pillars in my father's house, so did Audrey in mine. All of the qualities that I had been so entranced with on the 1934 tour to Palestine shine as constantly today as they did then and have through all the intervening years, during the beautiful times and the trying times. Without this remarkable woman of quiet strength and endless energy I know that none of my houses would have stood as strong and proud as they did.

It was during the eleven months that Audrey and I lived with Mother and Father on Somerset Street that I began to fully appreciate the depth and strength of Audrey Steinkopf Freiman. After less than two years of marriage, with the Depression threatening the very existence of the business that I was trying so desperately to learn, I had cut my salary, given up our cosy, furnished bungalow, and moved my beautiful dark-haired bride to the house of her in-laws. Looking back, I marvel that she didn't leave me then and there. Mother had objected to the idea, reasoning that no matter how sincere the effort, no household could live happily for very long with two strong-willed women under the same roof. But she had not yet come to know all of the qualities of this young lady from Winnipeg, via Toronto, who was poised and wise and patient—and very much her own person. Father was captivated, as was I, with Audrey's robust, yet thoroughly feminine, health and manner. Even then, despite her young age, she had a directness and frankness that were always disarming and a will that, if necessary, was unyielding. The youth of today speak of "getting it all together." Audrey "had it all together" then, as she does today.

In August 1941, our first child, Margo, was born. Four years later, in September 1945, our son A.J. arrived, and I watched our children grow in the same environment of unwavering love and wisdom that my mother had provided for me and my sisters. I think that the most important element in Audrey's and my years together is the genuine friendship that we share; we are husband and wife, lovers, parents of our children, and partners in the many things that interest us both.

80

There was much to do, and I approached the task with a confidence and certainty that reflected well on Father's training. Physically, the whole store bore the marks of the Depression and the "make-do" style of the war years. Father and I had discussed, in the weeks before his death, how to plan and proceed with the major face-lift that we knew was necessary if Freiman's was to "keep up with the times" and prosper.

We had contacted Raymond Loewy Associates of New York, the leading store design consultants in the US at that time, but had made no real progress on detailed planning. The shock of Father's death hung heavily on me for some time and it was not until the fall that I could turn my full energy and attention to the rebuilding job in the business.

After deciding in general terms what I wanted to accomplish, I retained Loewy Associates to redesign the entire street-level shopping area. While they were doing their planning and design work, I tackled the job of putting a new foundation under the entire store. The old logs that had held up the building for all those years could not take any additional weight – and I was determined to rebuild from the ground up. In the basement, each column was carefully cut, set upon jacks, and a new concrete base poured. The new steel was then joined. By the time that process was finished the architect's team was nearly ready to begin. That marked the beginning of a rebuilding, revitalizing program that spread over twenty years and involved architects and designers from New York, Los Angeles, Montreal, and Ottawa.

The physical remake was only the starting point. Our merchandise seemed to me sadly out of step with the new tastes and styles that literally exploded in North America after the war. I engaged Ketchum, Gina, and Sharp, a New York firm of merchandise consultants and architects, and with their help, and the skill of our buyers, we began to attempt to transform Freiman's into a smaller-city version of the legendary Bloomingdale's of New York. It was an exciting, busy time, filled with satisfying accomplishments. Financially, the business slowly prospered and we began to pay off the substantial arrears on the preferred stock.

By the early 1950s, the "suburbia phenomenon" was firmly entrenched in North America and the whole concept of city-centre retailing was being challenged by neighbourhood shopping centres. As I watched these developments in other cities, I knew it was only a matter of time before Ottawa, too, began to sprout suburban wings.

In 1954 we opened our first department store in Westgate, the first shopping centre in Ottawa. It was 60,000 square feet, and for me in particular, a pretty dangerous undertaking. We knew that Simpsons-Sears would soon open a large department store, of 160,000 square feet, further along the narrow strip of Carling Avenue. My hope was that the large shopping centre down the road would generate more traffic, help our much smaller store, and force the city into building a wider road to handle the heavy flow of new traffic. Whether we were courageous, foolish or lucky – or all three – I don't know, but everything turned out as we had hoped, and the store was soon selling more than we had budgeted for. A few years later the city widened the roadway to accommodate the heavy crush of traffic.

Ottawa's suburban growth was continuing and I wanted to be prepared for whatever the future might hold. In 1956 we bought forty-four acres in the east end of Ottawa, the corner of St. Laurent Boulevard and the Queensway. Believing it to be a logical location for shopping-centre development, I filed the plan under "hold for future development."

At about the same time, a new type of retailing that had originated in the United States popped up in Toronto – the discount department store. I decided that I had better learn what this was all about. Accompanied by our gifted controller, Fred Matatall, who more than anyone was my right hand and gave great strength where there could have been great weakness, I set off on a discount-learning tour of the US. Fred compiled the research of the discount stores we wanted to see, collected everything he could get for us to read, and we started off – Chicago first, and then east.

In each place we engaged a driver and car, saw the discount places, had dinner, and retired with our discount-department-store reading at night. By the time we got to Boston we were ordering fixtures. In a little over one year, we were building our second huge discount store in Ottawa under our own label – Freimart Stores Limited – a wholly-owned subsidiary of Freiman's. These stores were totally competitive with Freiman's. Our strategy was to sell at Freiman's a qualitatively better merchandise than was available at Simpsons-Sears, our main Ottawa competitor, and at Freimart, a lower priced level of goods, thus never meeting Simpsons-Sears head on. From the beginning, with their knowledge of hard goods, acquired from the giant of them all, Sears Roebuck, and their know-how in soft goods, acquired from the Robert Simpson Company, Simpsons-Sears had outpaced everyone else in Canada.

Our discount stores were an immediate success, and we were making strides in our conventional stores as well. Now there were four: our main downtown store; Westgate; and two discount stores, one in the west end of Ottawa, and one in the east end. We were also proud that our comptroller, working with IBM and Sweda, had developed for us the most advanced electronic system in merchandising, and store executives from all over the United States were coming to see how we did it.

Yet, in the midst of those champagne days, it was clear that not everything was bubbly. K-Mart, the department store division of S.S. Kresge, was on the Canadian trail and Woolco, the department store division of Woolworth, was pressing. The Hudson's Bay Company was looking eastward, Eaton's and Simpsons were on the prowl. Lesser, but big companies, were beginning, and even though their merchandising operations did not appear to be threatening, Miracle Mart was talking about five or six department stores in Ottawa. And there was Sears, waiting to jump again; they were only in the west end, but it was obvious that eventually they would move to encircle the town. But life was good, and these things were simply part of the challenge and the fun of business in a booming economy.

I enjoyed most aspects of business, but the real treat for me always was the enchanting world of high fashion. For years I have been fascinated by the way fashion expresses the social, moral, and economic tone of each period.

In the twenties there was the "collegiate-flapper" look: young men in baggy, wide slacks, blazers, and wildly-coloured ties, and girls in tight sweaters, short, pleated skirts, or the sequined-spangled, above-the-knee, fringed Charleston dresses with no bosom. It was the era of the Stutz Bearcat, the college prom, the hip flask for the football games, racoon coats and pork-pie hats. It has been suggested that fashion then signalled the alleged breakdown of morals after the First World War.

In the Depression years of the thirties, and into the forties, conservative fashion returned. The collegiate look was over. Now, young men wore sensible sports jackets and "saddle" leather shoes. The girls wore plain-coloured twin sweater sets, longer skirts, and small pearl necklaces. This was the "uniform." Even "the mob" wore black ties and wide-brimmed black fedoras, and their "molls" wore long satin evening dresses with slits up the sides. Something of a return to the thirties' fashions occurred in the fifties. Young people were not sure of themselves because they were not sure of what society held for them. Their attitudes and their clothes reflected it.

And then came the sixties, and a protest against the styles of the "Establishment." If males of the Establishment were clean-shaven, wore ties and jackets, and shined their shoes, the youth of that period moved to long hair, beards, blue jeans, no ties, mini-skirts, and no bras. They symbolized the permissiveness of society in that era.

The early seventies brought a more conservative trend. The hippie style of the sixties disappeared and was replaced by a cleaner look. Young men's hair was longish and well-styled. Beards were on their way out, but when worn, were finely trimmed. Jeans and sports shirts were better tailored and better made. High fashion now reflects the more casual life of the seventies, but it also reflects a degree of elegance. There is a reflection, also, of a more conservative taste, partly created by inflationary prices, so that many women, even those who can well afford the prices, reject high-price items for more conservative and less expensive things. Some of them think it is poor taste and somewhat immoral to spend a great deal of money on, say, a small afternoon dress. This trend also accounts for a loss of the former, more formal, fashion authority. This high fashion look, as the way of life, is casual, but deceptively so.

My fascination with fashion comes naturally, I suppose. Father was keenly interested in it and I remember his endless discussions with my mother and sisters about fashion all during my youth. He took me to my first "opening" in Paris at the *haute couture* house of Martial and Armand when I was only nineteen.

I remember so well the beautiful girls modelling those expensive and glamorous dresses. All proceeded well for me until a small man with a white, waxed moustache arrived with a perfume atomizer and began to spray all and sundry. I ducked but he "got me," to my total embarrassment.

Some years after entering the business, I knew that Canadian interest in fashion would have to develop substantially before we could import from Europe in meaningful quantities. Soon after the Second World War, I felt that the time was right. I approached my friend, Arthur Kaufman, who was President of Gimbel's Philadelphia, and responsible for the buying offices in Europe of the Gimbel's-Saks Fifth Avenue group, and made arrangements to do our European buying through their offices. That was the beginning of one of the most pleasant sequences in my life.

Each trip was more glamorous than the one before. Paris, exciting and outrageously expensive, was always my favourite stop, mainly because the great skill of the couturiers never failed to excite me. There is a visible social history in *haute couture*. The generations of great taste and skill in the art of *haute couture* over the centuries were reflected always in what we saw at the Paris showings. One need only go back to the fabrics and designs of the gowns of Dubarry and Marie Antoinette to know that Yves Saint-Laurent, Chanel, Givenchy, and Pierre Cardin are not accidents, but the products of a continuity that flows from a grand fashion past. The French are people of great taste and elegance, and their clothes, as much as their food, wine, and architecture, reflect this historical fact.

Only in Paris would one find a buying office where the manager knew and cared at least as much about art as he did about fashion. This was Saks' manager in Paris. He was an art connoisseur who knew all the galleries and all the best prices. He was buying pictures for some of the best private collections in America. In those days, just after the war, he took me through his favourite small galleries and showed me pictures he wanted me to purchase, including a Vlaminck, a large oil with an eerie sky before a storm, and a church steeple. It was priced then at about $2,800. Roualt was selling at between $1,200 and $1,400. The price for a large racetrack watercolour by Raoul Dufy was

$1,400, and a large Renoir pencil drawing was about $1,200. It is hard to believe when viewed against today's astronomic prices.

I was experimenting with the European markets and buying many kinds of merchandise, including dresses, sportswear, lingerie, and all kinds of accessories. From the first showings, it was obvious that we could not buy much of the high fashion in France because of the extremely high prices. But we could buy the boutique lines, which are designed by the designers whose names they bear, but are usually made by somewhat lower-priced production houses. As I began to learn more about buying in Europe, a strategy was developing.

In the fall we held our first major import promotion with the theme "Freiman's Brings the World to Your Door." We assembled for that show a presentation of the finest couturiers from London – Hartnell, Cavanaugh, Hardy Amies, and others. With one of the most magnificent collections ever assembled, we held the showing at the Chateau Laurier, using as models the wives of various ambassadors to Canada. All proceeds went to the Red Cross, with Freiman's paying all expenses. It was a highly successful launching of a merchandising style that was to become a tradition and trademark of Freiman's.

In the summer of 1949, a few years after our happy association began with Gimbel's-Saks, Harold Perlmann, their general manager in Europe, came to spend a weekend at our summer place. His purpose was simple – and delightful. He had left Gimbel's-Saks and wanted to come with us. He served as General Merchandise Manager for the next twenty-three years until he retired. In 1956, we changed our buying arrangements in England by joining the office in London operated by Ohrbach's of New York, whose manager was George Baker.

George Baker was charming, thoughtful, and gracious. His first thought was always of his client, to whom he gave every consideration. He always arranged for the same suite for me at the Savoy, where every small detail was arranged in advance. Nothing seemed to be too much for him, including meeting aircraft at ridiculous hours, always impeccably attired with bowler hat and umbrella. He was a polite, reserved English businessman, but everyone who knew him well felt his warmth, wit, and kindness. The same chauffeur, Burbidge, was always on hand to take us through the countless places we visited in our usual four-day rush through the English market. If there was a typically splendid British chauffeur, Burbidge was he. He accomplished everything he had to do, but never appeared rushed. He had perfect manners, was a staunch Tory in his politics, and lived for his annual trip to Ascot where each year he was engaged to take friends of the royal party. The greatest moment of his life was the year good fortune arranged for him to drive Princess Margaret and her friends there. Burbidge was, of course, quite snobbish, particularly when it came to doormen of hotels, other chauffeurs, and British "bobbies." He told me one day what a shame it was that the Labour Government had made the tremendous mistake of developing housing for workers in a part of the West End. They had changed the atmosphere of the area entirely, and he felt that it should have been kept for people whom he believed should be there. British lords and ladies, in his view, were the only English people who really mattered.

We did well in the early days with London fashion, particularly with Frederick Starke, who was always most kind and generous. He was attractive, interested in the arts, and responsible for fashions of distinction at reasonable prices. His styles were neither extreme nor dull, but elegant and in good taste.

Another of our British designers was Hardie Amies, who was designing the Queen's dresses then and was a couturier to be reckoned with by any European standard. Besides Frederick Starke and Hardy Amies, we bought from Leslie Kaye, Jaeger, Harry Popper, Jean Muir, Susan Small, John Cavanaugh, and Norman Hartnell, all of whom brought to us the well-made, well-mannered fashion of London, which was quite different from that of the French and the Italian.

It was not long before we saw boys with long hair and girls with mini-mini skirts in London. My first reaction was that our young people would never "go" for them. I could not imagine Canadian boys wanting to look like girls or Canadian girls being "immodest" enough to wear the mini-minis. But I thought that we should at least test the idea.

Mary Quant was the "high priestess" of this new swinging British style of the early sixties and the Beatles were rapidly becoming the heroes of the emerging era for the young. She had her showroom in an old house when we visited her. We bought her things: mini-minis, the small, strange knits, and little berets to match. We saw the first high boots, which she showed but didn't sell, and which we wanted to buy for this new "total look." We did put it together, and were off on an exciting new youth program that heavily influenced the development of fashions for the young at Freiman's. It was obvious that the store could be only as good as the young people it could attract; otherwise the old would just become older, as would the store, and both would eventually die. This led to the development of larger junior departments, new departmental ideas, new kinds of fashion showings, all in tune with the swinging sixties.

Our usual European buying trip took us to London, then to Paris, and on to Italy. On the Continent, we had joined the American Export Company, whose stores included Ohrbach's, Bonwit Teller and I. Magnin. Mr. E. Zaretsky, proprietor of the Paris office, was a small man blessed with cool efficiency and graceful European charm. He personally made all the "proper arrangements," the right suite at the Ritz, the inevitable long-stemmed red roses on the Empire table in the living room. Regrettably, Mr. Zaretsky died only a few years after we joined the office in 1956. Felix Vercelles then took over. Felix was attractive, artistic, and a perfectionist. No day was complete without fresh flowers in his office. Extremely elegant, he was a gourmet who liked his chauffeur to wait outside the restaurant beside his chocolate-coloured Rolls-Royce. Felix's artistic passions prompted him to open art galleries in Paris and New York – both extremely successful.

During the years after the war I had chased around Europe myself, buying many kinds of merchandise. Realizing the need for more "depth" in this specialized field, I started in the late 1950s to take along our fashion co-ordinator, Mrs. Mary Kosalle, and our major sportswear buyer, Miss Marie Crossley. They quickly became experts on European buying and it was a joyous thing for me to see their authority in the markets of Europe.

In France, there was now emerging a new world of French fashion – "*prêt à porter*." Until the late fifties most people thought of Paris as a world of *haute couture*, but even then that world was changing. The American Export representatives attended all the *couture* showings and shopped all of the emerging ready-to-wear collections. We had the best of both fashion worlds. I was completely spoiled by "Les Girls" of the American Export staff, particularly Juliette, Lotte, and Simone. They made these trips a happy business experience and one in which each day held its own Parisien charm. Ricky, the office manager, spoiled me more than anyone about "any little thing" that I might require. "Les Girls" made certain that I would not go hungry. They knew of my predilection for good bistros and saw that each luncheon was arranged at a favourite one.

Little by little over the years, we found our way around. We found houses that made the boutique gowns of the big name *couture* collections. It was not long before such names as Pierre Cardin, Nina Ricci, Jacques Heim, Jean Dessés, Madeleine de Rauch, and Lanvin Castillo appeared in Freiman's advertisements. At the same time, we introduced to Ottawa the co-ordination of jewellery and accessories for which Paris is known. We bought the first see-through crocheted sweater-blouses to be worn without bras, thinking how daring we were and how, certainly, no one would buy them in Ottawa. How wrong we were! They were all sold in a matter of days.

We took as a principle that there could be no compromise with fashion. I was pleased to share the responsibility of any new look, no matter how extreme it appeared to be, with our fashion buyers. One went to Europe to buy fashion, and therefore, it would have been pointless to go there to buy things that were not high fashion. This seemed obvious, and yet, buying a completely new look in fashion required some daring.

After Paris, Italy was another world. In Florence, we were with the office of the late Count Georgini, an aristocrat whom Audrey thought was one of the handsomest and most charming men she had ever met. His palazzo was perfection, and it was there that he gave parties with impeccable taste. One would enter the great marble foyer, mount the exquisite circular stairway, and at the top be received by the Count and his enchanting Countess. Directly behind them was a small wall of roses and, behind that, the party in the great salon. The party was never large, and every detail and aspect was gracious perfection.

I particularly enjoyed seeing the hand-blocked printing done in small Italian factories. The fabulous colours of Pucci's silk prints could be produced only in Italy. These colours, Pucci's fashion authority, and his business ability combined to make his great success. When I visited his fine palazzo in Florence and saw his creations in these surroundings, I felt a sense of Italian artistic history being honoured even in the typical, small, brilliant dress, "the thing that Pucci does."

Certainly there cannot be a more important fashion experience than a showing at the Pitti Palace. After mounting the ancient majestic stairway of the palace to the salon with its great crystal chandeliers and broad runway, one could feel the excitement of a great fashion moment. Here were the significant fashion people of the world and some of the best indications of fashion trends in Europe.

And, of course, there was Simonetta. The first time I entered Simonetta's I was greeted by a loud jingle-jangle and the barking of dogs, emanating from the many bracelets she wore on both arms and the small white poodles that were literally bouncing around her exquisite showroom. Simonetta was a person of great taste, discernment, and creativity. Her high standards made her one of the great *couturières* of Europe. She was also one of the most stunning women I have ever met. On my first meeting with her, I did not have a fashion buyer with me and I asked her to choose the things that she thought might be best for us. She did so, and we did very well with her selection. The next time I was in Rome, I did the same thing again, with wonderful results.

Another impressive woman who began to gain acceptance for knits as extremely high fashion, was the Marquesa Mirsa. She was a woman of great dignity and knowledge, and one who commanded respect from the moment of first meeting.

We also enjoyed going into the showroom of the Fontana sisters. They were women of taste and great *joie de vivre*.

Then there were the young men, Mingolini-Gugenheim, who created a fashion furore in the excellence of their fabrics, the beautifully handworked materials and splendid design. Their dresses were extremely expensive but worthy of inclusion in any good collection.

There was also Baldini, whose models were all flat and rather boyish looking. One year he arranged a showing for my wife,

Mrs. Kosalle, and me. Mrs. Kosalle inquired as to what would happen if a lady with a bust wanted to buy one of these dresses. He threw his hands in the air in a frustrated Italian gesture of disdain and replied, "My dear, we don't make dresses for *those* kind of women." Anyone with a bust, in his opinion, was not chic, and he just couldn't be bothered with the whole thing.

In Rome, I would leave the Excelsior and sit on the Via Veneto for hours, soaking up the excitement of so many people. In Florence, I went for walks across the Ponte Vecchio, looking into jewellery stores and small galleries. At Harry's Bar in the evening there were always people to talk to and a friendly mood and climate that made it all enjoyable and memorable.

And there was New York. Over the years, it became almost a second home for me. It was not that we bought so much in New York markets or that I found them as exciting as those in Europe, although we had modest success with some of the better designers: Herbert Sondheim, Larry Aldrich, and, of course, with Sally Victor's gorgeous hats. New York is truly "that wonderful town." The Metropolitan Opera was and still is the best show in town.

In my view, New York theatre is more exciting than it is anywhere, including London. Most significant, however, is the particular and special contribution the United States has made to the performing arts. This contribution, singularly American, took the old-fashioned musical comedy to a new art form. Typical of this new movement were *Oklahoma!, Porgy and Bess*, and *West Side Story*. Oscar Hammerstein and Richard Rogers, combined with Agnes DeMille, created a new kind of musical experience in *Oklahoma!*. George Gershwin in *Porgy and Bess* brought a fine contemporary folk opera to the world. *West Side Story* brought together two of the greatest talents of our time. Leonard Bernstein and Jerome Robbins created a score and choreography for contemporary ballet that brought about a new artistic dimension to the musical.

New York is a place of friendship and adventure. Jack Kriendler's and Charlie Berns' 21, a sophisticated place with fabulous food, was also warm and comfortable for me, much more of a club than my own club in New York. Monte, who was married to one of the Kriendler sisters, would be at the door. In the old days all of the Kriendler brothers–Jack, Mac, Bob, and Peter–would pleasantly descend upon you. Jerry Berns would be there, and with luck, Charlie Berns would amble by. At 21 there was an ambience at once happy and yet sophisticated, knowledgeable, and amusing. Over the years, it was great to drop in after work around 5:30 and talk to the boys before their early dinner together, and meet whoever happened to be around.

One day at 21, chatting with a good-looking gentleman with a thin, droopy moustache, unshaven face, and not-very-clean sneakers, I complained about the terrible flight I had had from Los Angeles. In those days, one flew in a DC-3. The flight, which made many stops along the way, took from 7:30 P.M. Los Angeles time to 12:30 P.M. the next day, New York time. The gentleman asked what airline I had used, and I told him TWA. He next asked what was wrong and I described the meals in detail. He then signalled for a telephone at our table and the operator, who knows the voice of every regular customer, immediately got his office on the phone. Only then did I realize that this Mr. Hughes, to whom I had been introduced, was the legendary Howard Hughes and that he owned the airline. I heard him arrange for a meeting the next day at 11:00 to correct these matters. It was obvious that he was totally in command, a perfectionist, and capable of making quick decisions on all matters, none of which was too small to attend to in his vast enterprises.

Peter Kriendler of 21 has been my close friend over the years. Our custom was to fish together about sixty-five miles north of Ottawa at the Hincks, the lodge of our mutual friend, Dr. Charles Shapiro. Dr. Shapiro was known to almost everyone in the theatrical world because from his early youth he had a fascination for people connected with the theatre. People would come from New York and all places west, particularly Hollywood, to fish at Charlie and Rose's. It was there that Gabriel Pascal came after inducing George Bernard Shaw to permit him to do a film of *Pygmalion*. One day, Pascal wanted to cook his special Hungarian goulash, and sent a messenger all the way to the city for one shaker of paprika. Regrettably, his speciality did not turn out to be a gourmet masterpiece. I also remember hearing sad stories from one of the greatest of contemporary comedians at that time, the late Bert Lahr, when he visited at the Hincks with his lovely wife, Mildred. He was sad and neurotic, but greatly loved despite his idiosyncracies because he was gentle, affectionate, and thoroughly artistic. One never knew who would arrive for the weekend. There were the nightclub owners whose wives had been Ziegfeld Follies girls years ago, distinguished investment bankers, or just plain movie folk.

Fishing with Peter K. was always a great experience. Herbert Hoover, in his small book on the subject, said fishermen had to be the ultimate optimists, or they would never go fishing. Peter was always sure that the next catch would be the "big one." One day it was, and he hauled in a twenty-six-pound northern pike. I was overwhelmed both by his ability and by the size of the fish. By chance, I happened to be in New York a couple of days later, went to 21 to dinner with Pete and was delighted to see on the menu "Northern Pike à la Hincks." We were told later that there had been only two orders for Pike à la Hincks – and those from Peter and me. The sauce was delicious, but even 21 couldn't remove the countless small bones that are embedded in a northern pike. Lunching with Peter at 21 was always something I looked forward to with great anticipation. No matter how elegantly dressed, he always managed to retain the look of a true sportsman with his radiant smile and year-round tan. One of the most distinguished fishermen in America, Peter has deep-sea fished around Bimini, in the Caribbean, and in the North Sea. He has killed salmon in Sweden and in Scotland.

Peter still tells the story about the day I met Zsa Zsa Gabor:

Lawrence, looking around the bar, spotted this most beautiful woman – "Pete," he said, "I know that lady. I can't remember where I met her." He was quite puzzled but positive that he knew her. Finally, to convince him, I went over to the lady whom I knew and asked her would she mind coming over to the bar because my friend said he had met her and knew her. She came right along and I introduced Zsa Zsa to Lawrence. Well, that convinced him that she was now a new friend – he invited her to lunch and then and there, a new friendship started.

It is strange that we feel we know people we have seen on television or in the movies. Miss Gabor was charming and told me she was going to Toronto to appear on "Front Page Challenge" the following week with my good friend from Ottawa, Fred Davis. She invited my wife and me to see the program and join her current husband, herself, and Fred after the show. Unhappily, her great charm was outweighed by a heavy work schedule that made it impossible for us to go to Toronto. It was our loss, because Zsa Zsa's *joie de vivre*, wit, intelligence, and beauty are memorable.

Business during these years was as interesting as it was hectic. The speed of everything was increasing and a revolution was beginning in decor and design. In 1963 I made frequent trips to Los Angeles, where I felt that some of the stores had created brighter and happier environments than any found in Canada or in the eastern United States. There I engaged Welton Becket and Associates, an outstanding firm of architects. In April 1964, the plans for a more contemporary and comfortable Freiman's were completed, and we started yet another round of redevelopment.

Business went well. Sales and earnings climbed steadily and we looked around for new challenges. In 1964, Simpsons-Sears approached us with a proposal for a development in Ottawa's east end. They were interested in the forty-four acre site that we had purchased back in 1956. After a series of meetings with their Chairman, Jack Barrow, their President, at that time, Jim Button, and their Vice-President in charge of development, Morgan Reid, we flew in their aircraft over the city, studying the growth and development patterns and concentrating on the east end. Then we dined sumptuously in their large suite, where the Simpsons-Sears team proposed that together we develop a shopping centre, with theirs and Freiman's as the anchor stores, thus creating the first regional shopping centre in the national capital.

I was concerned that the east end of Ottawa would not have enough population for some years to support such a centre and that, without it, a large east-end centre would only jeopardize our downtown business. Simpsons-Sears wanted a department store in the east end of Ottawa as soon as possible. If we did not want to participate, they made it quite clear that they would purchase another property and develop a shopping centre themselves. Because one-department-store shopping centres were rapidly becoming obsolete, I assumed that the prospective partner could only be one of the large ones. I had been offered a "Hobson's choice!" With misgivings that it might well be too early for us, I agreed and the plans to build the stunning St. Laurent Shopping Centre were announced in a joint release on December 4, 1965.

St. Laurent became and is a splendid shopping centre. I believe that our store there, designed by architect Daniel Schwartzman of New York, is one of the best-designed department stores of its kind anywhere. My misgivings about it being too early had been at least partly correct and in the first year, it did not do as well as we expected. Our expenses, including high development costs, were higher than we had planned and this large, attractive shopping centre was undoubtedly siphoning off some of our downtown sales. But gradually, as the area population grew, sales and earnings steadily improved and the long-term success of the venture was never really in question, despite the surge of newly-arrived competitors such as K-Mart, Miracle Mart, a new Woolco, a smaller Ogilvy's department store, Leon's Furniture Store and other of the large new specialty variations, including Canadian Tire and Bad Boy. But the new competition simply made us work that much harder, and we held onto our leadership role and expanded our share of the market.

From the end of the war to the sixties was the most gratifying period of my business life. We had weathered and learned from the harsh lessons of the Depression and of the war that followed. The economic up-and-down cycles notwithstanding, business moved at a dizzying pace and change followed upon change with a speed that was at times difficult to see. The house of Freiman continued with a style and strength that would have pleased Father. This period had been a time of fulfillment, but there had been moments of great distress, too.

Chapter VI

I Remember:

A Phone Call

The ringing phone awakened me instantly and I moved quickly to the sitting room of our suite in Winnipeg's Fort Garry Hotel, trying to pick up the phone before it awakened Audrey. It was 3:15 A.M. on June 2, 1961, and we were in Winnipeg for the funeral of Audrey's mother, which had been conducted the previous day. The caller was Fred Mattatal, our comptroller, and his first words told me how deeply upset he was. He had just been informed that the police had uncovered a well-advanced plot to kidnap our son, A.J. The RCMP later confirmed that an undercover agent had infiltrated a gang of five hardened criminals that operated in the Ottawa area and had learned of their plans to kidnap A.J. and hold him for ransom. The attempt was to be made that Thursday when A.J. walked home from school. I thanked Fred for telling me so promptly, put the phone down and forced myself to pause and think. I walked quietly into the bedroom, to ensure that Audrey was still sleeping. I was startled to find her sitting on the bed, extension phone still in her hand. She had heard the entire conversation. She looked at me steadily, and asked, with a calmness that told me she was in total control of herself, "How soon can we be home?"

The newly-wed Freimans return to Ottawa from New York.

November 1918, an eight-year-old Lawrence joins in the Armistice Day celebration in the back seat of the car at 5:00 A.M.

A young Lawrence at Meach Lake with an early morning catch.

Dominating the 1925 store window is the famous four-thousand-pound cake for Freiman's annual birthday sale.

Family portrait taken at sister Queene's wedding reception at the Meach Lake home. (Left to right) sister Gladys and Bernard Alexandor, their daughter Betsy, sister Dorothy, Audrey and Lawrence, Lillian and Archie Freiman, the bride, and groom Ben Luxenberg. PHOTO BY YOUSUF KARSH

On a donkey, with Queene and Audrey astride camels, outside of Cairo, on the trip during which Audrey and Lawrence met.

Queen Elizabeth visits the site on which the National Arts Centre is being built. Prime Minister Pearson is seated to the Queen's right. PHOTO BY JOHN EVANS PHOTOGRAPHY LTD.

A glass of champagne with Frances Hyland after a performance at the National Arts Centre of *The Ecstasy of Rita Joe*. PHOTO BY JOHN EVANS PHOTOGRAPHY LTD.

With Audrey, John Diefenbaker, and his wife Olive, at a formal reception in Ottawa.

Talking with Israel President Ben Zwi when Lawrence Freiman and Samuel Bronfman led the first Canadian mission to Israel.

Golda Meir and Audrey greet each other at a reception for Mrs. Meir at the Chateau Laurier.

Leading the Ottawa Philharmonic in an amateur conducting competition, a fund-raising event, at the Coliseum. PHOTO BY TED GRANT

Donning his costume for the "Springtime Parties" event—a production of *Peter and the Wolf*. PHOTO BY NEWTON.

Workmen putting up the sign changing Mosgrove Street to Freiman Street.

We caught a 6:00 A.M. flight to Toronto, made a close connection to Ottawa, and arrived just before noon. I went straight to the police station while Audrey went home to A.J. I was utterly appalled when I learned how the police had planned to apprehend the would-be kidnappers. They proposed to use A.J. as a decoy, having him walk as usual along the Driveway from school. Armed policemen would be hidden all along the route and they would grab the gangsters the moment they made their move. I flatly refused to co-operate, terrified at the thought of what could happen if armed policemen challenged the kidnappers who, undoubtedly, would be armed.

I was equally determined that we would all continue to function as normally as possible. A.J. was in the midst of final exams at school and I decided that he would complete them come hell or high water. I consulted my old friend Charles Roney, who operated Universal Investigation, a private security firm. He agreed to provide personal protection 'round the clock for A.J., who would be driven to and from school. The police co-operated fully, the RCMP, Ontario Provincial Police, and Ottawa city police each providing extra protection in their respective jurisdictions. RCMP Commissioner Harvison was especially concerned that the press would publish the story, and he feared repercussions from such publicity. I called my friends in the press and explained the situation to them; to a man, they agreed to co-operate. The days that followed were tense and fearful, but A.J., although only sixteen, conducted himself with remarkable bravery. Then, after about a week of wearying tension, the Toronto *Telegram* broke the story. The Ottawa press could hold their silence no longer and our lives became a circus of inquisitive reporters and determined photographers. At last, the nightmare came to an end. The RCMP assisted us in our plans for leaving and as soon as A.J. completed his last exam we took Margo and A.J. and headed off on a trip through Europe. We were pre-boarded on a flight to London, where we picked up a car, drove to Folkestone, crossed to France, and continued on to Switzerland. We spent a couple of weeks in Grindelwald, motored to Zurich, and flew home.

The first thing I did on arriving home was to call Commissioner Harvison. He told me, with obvious relief, that the matter had been resolved, and that we could relax and enjoy life as usual. He said that he wanted to have a chat with A.J. and asked if I would bring him around to his office the next day. I did, and the Commissioner spent a full hour explaining to A.J. why he should have no further concern about his safety. It was a thoughtful, touching gesture by a kindly man, and there is no doubt in my mind that the Commissioner's logical reassurances were an important contribution to A.J.'s peace of mind.

A Letter

A few years later, in 1964, another episode brought frightening clouds into our lives. Thomas Patrick Terrence Dooley had been my private secretary for over thirty years. His thoughtfulness over the years had thoroughly "spoiled" me. He had that infectious smile, wit, and joviality, that only the favoured Irish can possess. He gave even more affection and love than he received from all who knew him. On this particular Thursday in the last week of June, there was no smile and no greeting when he brought in my mail. His face was ashen and he said simply, "Please read this letter that I have put on top of your mail." With that, he turned and walked out of the office. I read the letter at least three times, growing more incredulous with each reading:

Dear Mr. Freiman:

If you have opened this letter in the presence of others, continue it in privacy as the contents must remain in the strictest confidence.

Our organization must obtain considerable sums of money from time to time, in order to develop or expand our interests in various localities. Since these funds cannot be accounted for to government or other agencies, for a variety of reasons, we have had to resort to other means of providing them. The method of overcoming this obstacle is quite simple and most effective.

We assess a selected number of prominent businessmen in the area wherein our immediate interests are centered, offering them an attractive proposition: –that we trade them their lives for a specified amount of money in return. It is not surprising, therefore, that we have had remarkable co-operation and success over the years in dealing with our clients; offering them the retention of a precious commodity at a reasonable price. Who can better judge or weigh the value of continued life than the individual himself, facing the loss of it, who finds the purchase both necessary and reasonable. Anxious to complete it, he considers that he has made a wise investment.

Mr. Freiman, we are not an anti-racial or religious group, nor do we have any political aspirations, although we do dabble in politics from time to time, furthering our own interests. This is not the morbid effort of a crank, or cranks. It would be most unwise and personally disastrous for you to consider this proposition a bluff, as you cannot return from the grave to second-guess or negotiate. Only those left behind would mourn you and regret your rash stupidity. You must remain alive to earn, lose or enjoy financial wealth.

After investigation of the assets of the Freiman interests, we have fixed the amount of one hundred and twenty-five thousand dollars ($125,000.00) as the sum of money that you will deliver to us in return for sparing your life, or the life of one of the members of your family. This offer is final and binding, not subject to negotiation. There will be no future demands on our part. We expect your complete co-operation in this matter as well as your complete and eternal confidence. Failure on your part to honour these stipulations will cost you your life, even had you already bought and paid for it.

We must caution you further, Mr. Freiman, not to reveal this letter, or its contents to a living soul. Not to family, friends, business associates; financial, legal or spiritual advisors; nor to the police, the judiciary, or any group or individual in the legislative field. It would be futile to appeal to the authorities for help or protection; as it is such an uncertain and temporary assurance at best. Should you resort to such a move, we would bide our time, meanwhile concerning ourselves with other interests. After some time; months, perhaps, even years, the authorities, though promising differently at the outset, would gradually withdraw, ceasing protection of you and all the members of your family, placing you in a vulnerable position once again. At that time we would fulfill our promise, completing our business with you. Hiring professional protection would prove most ineffective and expensive over an indefinite period; in time the cost would exceed our original demand.

As far as fleeing the country or going into hiding is concerned, it would be well for you to realize that we have a reciprocal working agreement with sister organizations throughout the world; that they would co-operate most readily in locating or liquidating you, or any member of your family, should we place your names on the list.

As you can perhaps perceive by now, Mr. Freiman, our operation is most simple, direct and practical. We have carried it out many times over the years with complete success. Only twice have we had to order an execution due to hedging and appeals for time or further negotiation. In this day and age it is not a difficult matter to get to a man or his family with a sniper's bullet, a bomb, poison or the numerous other effective means of extermination known to the professional assassin. There are many depraved souls willing and eager to kill for money. Their methods are exacting, scientific and effective. We are in a position to contact them indirectly without revealing our identities or that of our organization.

Although we dictate the terms of this transaction, we must follow through on our half of the bargain. We honour them in that you will never be approached again in future when you have fulfilled our demands for the specified amount of money; followed our instructions to the letter regarding its preparation and delivery; plus your bond on eternal silence. We honour them in that we will cause your death, or that of one of your family, should you default in any way at this time, or at any time in the future. We must carry this out, otherwise the rumour might be circulated to different interested groups that our threats are empty and meaningless. Subsequently we would not remain in business too long after that.

Our reasons for going into such detail regarding our operation and your instructions which follow, are most valid and necessary. Since there will be no further communication, we must impress upon you at this time, Mr. Freiman, the fact that however unjust or unreal our demands might appear to you, it still remains a fact also that you must deal with us on our terms; otherwise you or one of yours will forfeit a life. There is no compromise.

Here are your instructions which you will study carefully and follow as they are outlined:

1. On Tuesday, June 30, you will insert an advertisement in the personal column of the *Toronto Daily Star*, to run one day only [exact wording was stipulated]. Placement of this advertisement will signify that you will comply with our terms exactly as specified. Failing to see this advertisement as outlined in the above mentioned newspaper, we must assume that you do not intend to heed us, therefore forcing us to carry out our part of the proposal. . .foreclosure on your life or one other dear to you should you temporarily elude us.

2. Having placed this advertisement, you must now prepare the required sum of money. We have purposely allowed you approximately one month so that you will be able to gather it together in as discreet a manner as possible, so as to avoid arousing suspicion in dealing with bankers, brokers, business colleagues, etc., as to the real reason of your need. You will obtain this money in denominations of fifty and/or one hundred dollars, banded in packets of twenty-five hundred dollars each. Do not keep any records of this currency. It would serve no beneficial purpose as we have stipulated that if anyone is apprehended in any way, at this or any future time, by reason of obtaining or using this money; we shall consider that you have defaulted and act accordingly. When we have received the currency, an expert will examine it for its authenticity, as well as to determine if it has been invisibly marked or otherwise treated for detection.

3. At some time previous to July 20, you will purchase a recent model station wagon in excellent mechanical shape. In the Cars For Sale section of the Monday, July 19, *Toronto*

Daily Star classified advertisements you will list this vehicle for sale for one day only as follows:

"Year, Make, Model, Colour, Licence No., Reasonable for cash [name and telephone number to be listed, was specified].

4. You will pack the money in a new brown leather Gladstone type bag, or two if necessary due to the greater amount being in small denomination. Lock the luggage securely.

5. Prepare the automobile in the following manner for Friday, July 24:

A. Automobile registration card in glove compartment.

B. Lower rear seat, or seats of vehicle, converting this area to deck-space and place the luggage containing the money on this surface.

C. You will place a spare set of ignition keys in a magnetic key container, such as may be purchased at any automotive supply store. Upon arriving at your destination, which will be designated in the paragraph following, you will affix this key container to the underside of the right rear bumper of the automobile, checking to make sure that it has engaged securely.

D. Arrive at destination with fuel tank approximately full of gasoline.

6. You will drive the automobile to the Yorkdale Shopping Plaza, at Dufferin Street and Highway 401 in Toronto. You will park it anywhere in the shoppers' parking area before noon, Friday, July 24. Lock the vehicle with your own set of keys, leaving the spare set beneath the right rear bumper as described above. Walk across the Plaza toward the stores before engaging transportation elsewhere.

7. Do not linger to watch the automobile in any manner, nor hire or instruct anyone else to do so; it will be picked up sometime before 9:00 P.M. on that day.

8. If you have followed these instructions exactly as they

were given, Mr. Freiman, your half of the transaction has been completed to our satisfaction. All that remains on your part is to destroy this letter completely and never reveal its contents to anyone at any time in the future. In doing so, your continued life is assured.

Within a few days after the pick-up you will be notified where the automobile may be recovered. This act on our part is our way of letting you know that we are satisfied with your performance to date and in keeping your own counsel, you will never hear from us again. It is our method of tendering you a receipt paid-in-full.

In order to further impress upon you the exactness of our operation and the futility of attempting to foil us in any way; we will describe roughly what takes place after you leave the automobile in the parking lot.

One of a number of innocents, who though carefully screened, are led to believe they were chosen at random, will pick up the automobile at Yorkdale Shopping Plaza. Ignorant of the true nature of the operation, they will be approached by an intermediary who is also unaware of the reason why he is selecting these drivers.

Ostensibly, the drivers are hired to return a vehicle belonging to a salesman who became ill while making a call and could not complete his trip. Each driver is given one torn half of a unit of currency, plus a small amount of expense money. He is told where the car is located, given a full description as well as where he may find the keys, and told where to deliver the vehicle. If he completes this errand to our satisfaction, the other half of the torn bill will be mailed to him. The process is repeated in exactly the same manner with yet another driver, and another; each man leaving the keys where he found them, after locking the automobile securely.

This process is repeated from points A to B to C, etc., until we are satisfied, having scrutinized proceedings from the guidelines, that the vehicle is not being watched, or followed along the route taken, or from the air; that you have indeed met our terms in every respect.

When we do finally take over the automobile it will be carefully checked immediately for transmitters, cameras, alarms, recording or other detection devices. It will also be tested for chemical treatment or dusting. Since all of our associates never congregate in the same place at the same time, if one or more of our number were apprehended in any manner, those remaining would make the arrangements for dealing with you.

When we have satisfied ourselves that both the automobile and the contents are clean; that the money is satisfactory in every respect; that no attempt has been made at providing for future detection, we will notify you where the automobile may be recovered. You have retained a set of keys for this purpose.

At that point, Mr. Freiman, our business is completed. Meet these terms...follow our instructions as they are given here...and you live. Disregard them, take action against them or ever break the silence and you, or other members of the Freiman family die...Violently.

We trust in your good judgement and desire for continued life.

Yours anonymously,
The Organization.

The phrasing, the hints of an international organization, the audacity of the concept—all told me that the danger was real. Phrases like "considerable sums of money," "interests in various localities," "a variety of reasons," and "other means" all conveyed an impression of cool confidence. Here was a shocking business proposition: "a wise investment" for "a precious commodity." I was being offered my life and the safety of my family for a given sum of money. My name had been placed "on the list" of this organization with sister organizations throughout the world, a terrifying family of criminal power and organization. Concerned as I was, I had to admire the practical simplicity of the letter. Its style was perfect for the purpose and there was the *honour* of the promise that would be kept to preserve the honourable business reputation of the operation. There could be no compromise.

I called Tom on the intercom and asked him not to disturb me. After about half an hour of the most serious thinking, I

112

called the Commissioner of the RCMP, George B. MacClellan, explaining that I had received a threatening letter and that I was inclined to take it seriously. I said that I had received "crank" letters before but something about this one worried me and I would be grateful if one of his colleagues could take a look at it. If they decided that it was unimportant, that would be splendid; but if they thought it was serious, I wanted to be advised what steps should be taken. I also said that in view of the possibility that it might be serious, I did not think it intelligent for me to take the letter to RCMP headquarters. The Commissioner agreed and said that he would send a plainclothes officer over immediately to pick up the letter. They would study it and contact me soon.

A few days later, Tom Dooley informed me that a gentleman was waiting to see me. He was shown into the office and identified himself as a senior officer in the RCMP. He told me that after studying the letter, he and his colleagues took the threat most seriously and they believed that careful steps must be taken to apprehend the person or persons involved. A direct telephone line to RCMP headquarters was installed in my office. It had been decided that there would be complete secrecy in the investigation – only those who had to would be involved. The days that followed were a confusing mixture of exciting involvement and flashes of adventure. I rented from my friend Charlie Belisle of Belisle Motors, a 1961 Chevrolet Corvair "Greenbriar." The RCMP believed this was a satisfactory model because the brown leather gladstone placed in the rear area would be clearly visible from outside the vehicle, but to retrieve it a person would have to climb inside the station-wagon – creating potentially valuable extra seconds at the scene.

On July 7, I met with the police in a room, the number of which was given on a private line, in the Chateau Laurier. There I was told of the plans that the police had made up to this point. I was asked about my personal day-by-day routine and business habits so that they could make final preparations. I brought to this meeting a second letter, which I had received that morning:

Dear Mr. Freiman:
A strike by the Typographical Workers Union against the

113

three major Toronto daily newspapers appears imminent. Although management has stated that they will continue publishing despite this action, there is some doubt that they will be able to fulfill all their commitments especially in their classified advertisements department. In order to avert the possibility of error or omission regarding the placements of your advertisement as ordered for July 20, you will have it published in [here a specific newspaper was designated] on the above mentioned date. The wording of the ad will remain unchanged with one exception...you will end the insertion with a local district telephone number of your choice or invention. All other terms and conditions as previously instructed.

THE ORGANIZATION

The police plan was elaborate and highly detailed. I was to be assisted by an officer in preparing and inserting the required want ad for July 20. The advertisement of June 30 had already been placed. I was to purchase a gladstone bag and my bank manager was to be told in general terms why I was withdrawing the money. I was then to make reservations at a Toronto hotel for the night of July 23. Police officers would be in an adjoining room for my protection during the night I was to stay in Toronto.

In the meantime, the officers to whom I had turned over the station-wagon had returned to Toronto and fitted it with an electronic device that would short-circuit the ignition by means of a radio signal. So it was that on July 23 at about 3:45, I was to leave the store for my trip to Toronto. A taxi was waiting at the rear of the store. The driver, in shirt sleeves and a small cigar butt in his mouth, was, of course, an RCMP officer. He proceeded to the bank which was just around the corner. In front of the bank were three gentlemen who appeared to be surveyors. I was informed later that they were police officers, stationed there for security reasons. The taxi was parked outside. I went inside to the manager's office. He proceeded to the rear of the bank and brought to his office $125,000 in cash. He made sure that my account was debited with this amount. All of this was done so that, should the extortionist have an accomplice in the bank, they would believe that the actual money had been placed in the gladstone bag. In

114

the manager's office, the real money was put securely into a small vault. The RCMP had left with him packages of paper the same size as the money and weighted so that the bag would weigh the same as if it contained $125,000 in small denomination bills. I carried the bag out to the taxi. As we drove to the airport, my RCMP taxi driver said, "If you hear a bullet, quickly lie down flat on the floor."

I replied, "If I hear a bullet, I'll lie down so damn fast you'll have no cause to worry."

We both laughed, but I got the message: whoever was behind this bizarre affair did not have to wait until the following morning to implement their plan. They could make their attempt at any time.

There was to be an RCMP officer or officers at the airport who would identify me by an Air France flight bag I was to carry. They had also been given photographs of me. Before I left home that morning, Audrey, knowing nothing of the whole situation, could not understand why I wanted to take an Air France flight bag; I had never taken a flight bag in my life. Neither could she understand why I was not staying at the Royal York. I had chosen a motor hotel quite a way out of the city. I told her that because it was warm, the meeting I was to attend was called at that hotel. It had a swimming pool and would be more pleasant. The real reason the police chose this hotel was that it was out of the city and the closest hotel at that time to Yorkdale Shopping Centre. They believed there would be less risk in my trip from the hotel to Yorkdale the following morning.

There was RCMP security on the aircraft, at the Toronto airport, and when I called a taxi, I knew I was being followed by another with police officers in it. We went to the hotel and as I entered my room, an adjoining door opened and I was greeted by two plainclothes police officers. They said that if I did not mind too much, the adjoining door would have to be open from that point on. I was told that during the night, while one officer slept, the other would stand guard. I was also informed that the day before, all personnel involved, including officers of the RCMP and the Metropolitan Toronto Police, had been thoroughly briefed. The key to the operation was special radio equipment, which was to be carried in a small "beaten-up" blue truck. The

115

"battle plan" for apprehending the extortionists was extremely detailed, and involved mobile teams who would patrol their areas in unmarked automobiles equipped with three-way FM radios tuned to a special frequency.

All together seven teams had been assigned, including another electronics technician and a technician from the RCMP who would be in another vehicle in the shopping centre. They would be ready to operate the electronic device in the station-wagon that I was to drive if and when required. Various detectives, some accompanied by policewomen, and all dressed to look like casual shoppers, patrolled the shopping centre. These "shoppers" used different kinds of shopping and other bags that contained walkie-talkies. My instructions were painstakingly detailed. I was to leave the hotel at 8:30 A.M., get in the station-wagon and follow the small blue truck at a respectable distance to Yorkdale. Unmarked police cars would be ahead of and behind me. At the shopping centre, I was to park the station-wagon in a place specified by the police, a spot in view of a vacant store that fronted on the parking lot. In the store was a movie camera and a portable radio receiver and transmitter. I was to arrive at approximately 10:00 A.M.

After my briefing, I slept surprisingly well, but greeted the morning tense and anxious to get the thing over with. I shaved and showered, had some coffee while I dressed, and left the hotel at 8:30 sharp. Everything proceeded as planned. When I arrived at Yorkdale, I parked in the allocated space, got out, locked the door and placed the key in the magnetic container under the rear bumper. I then walked, feeling unusually calm, toward the stores. As arranged, a taxi bearing a certain number arrived. A lady got out, I hailed the taxi and got in. The lady was, of course, a policewoman and the driver was a police officer. He took me back to the hotel where the two officers continued their security watch. We settled down to await further developments.

Back at Yorkdale, anyone who appeared near the station-wagon was considered suspect and was photographed by the camera equipment. A little after 4:00 P.M., a man who had been seen earlier near the station-wagon returned. He took the magnetic key keeper from the rear bumper, removed the key, opened the left front door, got into the vehicle and started the motor. The camera recorded the whole sequence. The moment he started the engine, the order to short the ignition was given. At that instant, four officers, who had been nearby, surrounded the car, seized the man, and marched him quickly to the vacant store. Other police watched carefully to see if any accomplices were involved.

The swift action by the police so overwhelmed the captive that he confessed on the spot and said that he alone was involved. When he was searched, half of a ten-dollar bill was found, apparently intended to prove his innocence if he were taken by police. Apparently, because of the speed of his arrest, he forgot all about it. Later, the other half of the ten-dollar bill was found in the man's home, as was the typewriter on which he had typed the letter. Just before 6:00 P.M., RCMP Commissioner MacClellan called from Ottawa to tell me of the arrest. I expressed my deep gratitude and congratulations to the Commissioner and the many officers of the RCMP and the Toronto police.

That done, I phoned Audrey to tell her, for the first time, the real reason for my "business trip." I then called my friend Louis Rasminsky, who was then Governor of the Bank of Canada. The day before I left for Toronto, I had gone to see Lou at his office and had told him the whole story. I felt that there should be one person who knew the situation in case something went wrong. When I told Lou on the phone that the episode had ended satisfactorily, I could hear his deep sigh of relief. Equally relieved, I returned to Ottawa on the next plane.

It was later learned that the accused had lived in Ottawa for a time. The extortion scheme had been worked into a novel he was writing and he apparently became so intrigued with his plot that he decided to put it into action. He chose me as the target even though he did not know me. The accused pleaded guilty to a charge of attempted extortion and was sentenced to serve eight years in Kingston Penitentiary. At the trial it was revealed that he had served a previous term for armed robbery. The RCMP were obviously right in treating the threat of the first letter as a serious matter.

A Headline
Adversities usually come in clusters, and another deeply disturb-

ing situation developed while I was in the midst of the extortion affair. On the flight to Toronto to act out that nerve-wracking scenario, the stewardess handed me the Ottawa *Citizen* of July 23. Emblazoned in a large headline on the front page were the words: **Four Assault Club's Race Bar.** Included in the article was the following statement: "It is understood that Mr. Freiman, whose family have long been leading citizens of Ottawa, has been nominated for Rideau Club membership twice before. Both times he was 'blackballed,' apparently because he is Jewish."

I had never applied for membership–nor had I ever been blackballed.

After arriving in the Toronto hotel, with the Mounties in the next room, I was as distressed about this new problem as I was about the extortion situation. The facts were that at the annual meeting of the Rideau Club, which had been held shortly before the *Citizen* article appeared, the membership of the club decided that the membership rules would be changed. Recommendations of applicants, after being proposed and scanned, would in future go to a nominations committee. This committee would judge the qualifications of the applicant and, if found satisfactory, applicants' names would be posted. If any member felt that there were reasons why an applicant should not be granted membership, those reasons were to be submitted in writing to the committee. This meant that the "blackball" system of the past was finally done away with, because now justification for objection had to be given.

Immediately after this change in rules, Lou Rasminsky, David Golden, now President of Telesat Canada, and at that time Deputy Minister of Transport, my brother-in-law, Bernard Alexandor, and I were invited to join the club. We discussed the matter and concluded that it would be an impropriety not to join, because there was now a genuine desire to mend a situation that had long been discriminatory. We had, therefore, permitted our names to stand.

As soon as the Mounties had completed my hotel-room briefing on what I was to do at Yorkdale the next day, I placed a call to Robert Southam, publisher of the *Citizen*. I was told that he was at his country home on an island in the Rideau Lakes,

118

and did not have a telephone there. He could be reached if it was urgent through another telephone in the area. I felt there was great urgency because it was probable that unless something was done very quickly, The Canadian Press might pick up the story. In short order, Bob Southam was contacted on the island, took a boat to the mainland, and called me. He was deeply upset, because he had been unaware of the story. He promised to look into it immediately. Regrettably, parts of the story had been picked up by The Canadian Press, and I later found, to my horror, that the "blackball" error had been printed in several Canadian papers.

Around this time, I had been travelling extensively on behalf of the United Jewish Appeal. I was concerned that the Jewish people, so many of whom I had met in different cities of Canada, would believe that I had subjected myself to the indignity of wanting to join a club after being "blackballed," and I was frustrated at the thought of not being able to inform them that this was not true. I suppose I could have taken the matter to court, but I felt that this would only make the situation even more unpleasant, and I remembered too well the trauma of Father's court fight with Tissot. I expected a statement to be made by the club, which would clarify the situation. When this was not forthcoming within a week, I wrote the Secretary of the club requesting that my name be taken from the list of applicants. Shortly thereafter, the club published a most satisfactory statement and the public was told the true facts of the matter. I then advised the club to put my name back on the list. Not long afterwards, the memberships were accepted and the matter was closed.

Christopher Young was editor of the *Citizen* and a member of the Rideau Club. He conceded that he had seen the story before publication. He regretted the fact that the "blackballed" part had not been checked. He believed that in this matter the responsibility was the reporter's. He said, "The report on the breaking down of discriminatory barriers at the Rideau Club, which appeared in the *Citizen* was clumsy and badly-handled, but it was published from the best of motives in an effort to show the injustice of this kind of discrimination."

In retrospect, there is no doubt that this offensive situation resulted in a better understanding between people in the club, founded by Sir John A. Macdonald, well over a century ago. There is now empathy and understanding by a broader membership. It is gratifying to see gentlemen's clubs, such as this one, become clubs of gentlemen.

Chapter VII

My Search

From the earliest days I think that Father must have had a prophetic vision about the kind of city that Ottawa would become.
He moved to Ottawa in the first place because he "felt" that it
was home, the place where he wanted to live and work. I remember vividly walking with him one spring night when I was still in
grade school. It was exam time and after dinner, before beginning my studies, Father and I walked from Somerset Street,
down to the Driveway and along the Rideau Canal. The lilacs
were in full bloom and the spring air was sweetly heavy with their
fragrance. We stopped to admire the view along the canal.

"It was good that I came to Ottawa," Father mused. "It is so
very beautiful. You know of course, that's why I came here.
You're very lucky to live in such a beautiful place in this great
country." Neither of us could know then just how lucky I would
be for the privilege of being able to make some contribution to
this city.

"Altruistic egotism" is the term used by Dr. Hans Selye in his
book *Stress Without Distress*, to describe people who are self-
centred in working hard for themselves, but in so doing, receive
the understanding, sympathy, and respect of society for their

hard work and achievements. I do not know to what extent this motivation is applicable to my efforts. There was certainly the influence of and the good example set by Mother and Father. In any event, I do know that whatever the work involved in satisfying the material needs of people, there remains the further task of helping to provide a better quality of life through the continuous search for truth and beauty.

For these reasons, and to the degree that I might have helped, I want to look back at the years of the first orchestra in Ottawa; the theatre in Stratford; the close to eight years in the Federal District Commission (the predecessor of the National Capital Commission); and the basic planning of a national capital in which Canadians would eventually take great pride.

Also, I want to look back on my years and my happy association with the Oblate Fathers in the advancement of bicultural learning at the Université d'Ottawa, and subsequently on the years I spent when the university became a non-sectarian, provincial institution.

With all of this, there is also the need for social legislation to ensure the progressive well-being of Canadians. These considerations, over many years, were the concern of the Canadian Welfare Council, on which I had the honour of serving for two terms as president from 1953 to '55. (It is now the Canadian Council on Social Development.)

Finally, there is a fulfillment in having had the privilege of being the founding chairman of the National Arts Centre, which serves as a prideful institution of the performing arts for all Canadians.

Arts and Music
In 1944, I went to one of the first rehearsals of what was to become the Ottawa Philharmonic. After rehearsal, I invited the Concert Master Eugene Kash back to my house for a rare delicacy—corn flakes and milk and toast. I told him how extremely poor I thought the music was. Jack, which is what everyone called him then, as they do now, said it was my fault and the fault of all others who did nothing in their communities to support orchestras or the performing arts in general. He said, "How do you expect your daughter to grow up in a musical desert—the

122

capital of our country?'' I told him he was right, and I would try to do something.

I decided to use the store as the prime vehicle. The idea was that the company would sponsor pop concerts. So we engaged the orchestra, rented the old auditorium, and proceeded to plan our concerts, built around big-name performers. There was one admission price – one dollar. The concerts were a fine success. We had thousands munching hot dogs, listening to Jan Peerce or Alex Templeton, Militza Korjus, Conrad Thibeault, and so many more, and beginning to understand and appreciate fine music. And, of course, there were the wonderful parties after the concerts.

The orchestra gradually improved after a pretty grim start. Once Mario Lanza sang with the orchestra to an audience of around 400 people in the Capitol Theatre. As the orchestra improved, the audiences increased in size. We formed a ladies' committee, with Fiorenza Drew* as Chairman; she was active, charming, and enlisted the support of the senior diplomats' wives. She made things generally hum, and it was not long until the orchestra was artistically respectable. Soon SRO signs began to appear in the lobby.

There seemed never to be enough money, so we had "Springtime Parties." We booked the local cow palace, the Coliseum, and enlisted the support of well-known ladies and gentlemen to play in our "productions." One year we staged *Peter and the Wolf*, with full orchestra, and the old Coliseum was packed to the rafters. We invited Lorne Greene, who was born in Ottawa, to come from Hollywood to do the commentary and, in his full-voiced Hollywood manner, he produced a most dramatic rendition. Yousuf Karsh, the world-famous photographer, was Peter, and Charlotte Whitton, then Mayor of the city, was a not-too-graceful duck. I was the wolf, and a very over-heated one because I had a lot of running around to do with my extremely hot wolf's head and costume. His Excellency the Governor General Vincent Massey opened the proceedings and enjoyed the Springtime Parties as much as or more than anyone there.

*Fiorenza, the wife of the Leader of the Opposition, George Drew, was the daughter of the late Edward Hart Johnson, the former General Manager of the Metropolitan Opera.

Another time we had an amateur conductor's evening with full orchestra. I had long harboured a secret ambition to stand all-powerful, baton in hand, directing the orchestra to unheard-of musical heights. My fellow participants included the late Brooke Claxton, George Drew, Nicholas Monsarrat, and Mayor Charlotte Whitton. The conductor, Jack Kash, was to give each of us about twenty minutes of instruction, the orchestra would follow the direction of the "conductor," and there would be TV cameras, including one from the CBC national network. The "winner" was to be selected by an applause meter. Brooke Claxton won with ease. Rumour had it, however, that, as Minister of National Defence, he had the officer in charge of bands orchestrate a special martial version of "Alouette" and then made a recording of it. Rumour had it, also, that he rehearsed consistently and persistently with great vigour. When his turn on the podium came, he appeared with a small suitcase, opened it, took out a great, straggly, long-haired wig, placed it on his head, and began with a most professional downbeat, continuing his performance with great musical authority. When he finished there was a thunderous ovation. I was a poor second. I had changed my sports jacket for the maestro's tail coat. His arms were about half as long as mine, he could hardly find his violin under my long sleeves, and his short sleeves looked ridiculous on me. Musically, my performance left much to be desired. The particular part of Tchaikovsky I had chosen kept on erratically going faster and slower in all the wrong places. Nicholas, Charlotte, and George just couldn't make it come off at all, which is the only reason I made a poor second.

At the Springtime Parties, and other events, we worked hard and had incredible fun—and raised substantial amounts of money for the orchestra.

My involvement in the artistic life of Ottawa had really begun on my return from university in the early thirties. It was the beginning of a new learning experience. There were so many talented young people, mostly without jobs in those Depression days. A main gathering point was the home of Mr. and Mrs. Eric Brown, the Director of the National Gallery and his wife. They so enjoyed having young people around and pleasantly evoked discussions on art, music, and the theatre. The group included

124

Graham Spry, who with Alan Plaunt had written a brief on the development of the CBC, pursuing the philosophy that the air must be owned by all the people. Donald Buchanan in his over-quiet, endearing, and yet perceptive manner, spoke with knowledge and tenderness on the importance of developing Canadian artists in all art forms. Ross McLean was there with incisive brilliance and ever-ready smile and so were Peggi Nichol, the fine artist with impish laugh and strong talent, and Marjorie Borden, an artist full of cheer. And King Gordon talked of the Spanish Civil War: "The Fascists are coming. It is the beginning of the devil's world!" He later became Associate Editor of the *Nation.* Peter Aylen listened well, argued graciously, and loved to sit on the floor and play the panaphonic phonograph. Berlioz was his favourite. He went on to set up the International Service of the CBC, represented us in Ethiopia, and retired quietly to his books and friends under the warm, sun-lit skies of Jamaica. Bob Beatty, later Deputy Governor of the Bank of Canada, also enjoyed these gatherings as did Kay Fenwick. In those days we had so little money, but we enjoyed records, good talk, a few bottles of beer, and some cheese.

The old Edwards Lumber mill had been bought by the government as the home of what became the National Film Board. It was directed by Frank Badgely, the attractive, happy, easy-going Frank who treated all of his people with understanding and kindness. Soon it changed. Prime Minister King brought John Grierson from Britain to be Film Commissioner. The "wee Scot" was of tough fibre. He was a socialist of high intellectual principle, fair in his judgements, if not always correct, hard-drinking, and hard-working. His rumpled hair usually matched his rumpled attire – old tweed jacket and baggy "flannels." He inspired all of the young people there and encouraged them to do what *they* wanted to do. He was splendid – a great documentary film-maker. People of the calibre of Norman MacLaren emerged to their great artistic heights under his direction. Another film commissioner, Sidney Newman, felt Grierson's "touch" as did the composer-conductor, sensitive, and artistically strong-minded Lou Applebaum, presently Executive Director of the Ontario Arts Council. The Film Board in wartime under John's direction made fine films, and contributed to national unity by showing

Canadians what was being achieved in war by their own people.

Sometimes John G. would phone before I left the store to say, "Film Board next stop for you." I would obey, and he would take me to a screening room and show a film. We would repair afterwards to Madame Burger's fine inn in Hull for drinks and dinner and he would ask me to expound on the film. The premise was that I was the guy was paid at the box office. "To hell," John would say, "with all those experts and geniuses I have around me. Their job is to make 'em. You're the guy who has to look at them, so I've got to know what you think." Because I didn't know much about films, he valued my opinion.

Grierson "touched" my life as he touched others, people such as Guy Glover, Jim Beveridge, Bob Anderson, and Graham McInnes. Jim B. and Bob later made fine films and television shows. These were the years of development, creativity, and inspiration at the film board, and then everything began to go wrong–moving steadily from bad to worse.

In the United States there were the rumblings of McCarthy and Nixon, who had embarked on the Communist witch-hunt. It spilled over into Canada. An astonished John Grierson, who was also general manager of the Wartime Information Board, had to appear before the Canadian Royal Commission Enquiry into Espionage. But the crushing blow came to John G. when he had to forego a plan in the United States for an American "World in Action" series.

In 1945, Ross McLean was made Acting Film Commissioner under what he believed were difficult conditions–a much too small budget and staff. During the post-war years, his constant battle to expand was just as constantly thwarted, and he believed that the main reason was the charge that the Film Board harboured subversives. Even after a screening of all 800 of the staff by the RCMP, the allegation, in his opinion, lingered. In 1949, some of us saw Ross and his wife Beverly off at the station when he left for Paris to direct the film and visual division of UNESCO. He spent the next eight years there before returning to Ottawa to take up new duties, which eventually led to his being a consultant to the Canadian Radio-Television Commission on its policy and programing.

It was heartbreaking, after the heights of creativity and splen-

126

did morale, to see such hostility and distrust. One of my friends, whom I shall call Mr. "K," was a specialist in his field of film work and had decided that he could not work in the climate that existed then at the National Film Board. He accepted a position in the US, only to be turned back by their immigration authorities. No grounds were given but the implication was that he was a subversive. Under these circumstances, there was now nothing available to him in Canada. I went to the American Ambassador to Canada at the time, Laurence Steinhardt, and told him of the case. He agreed immediately to look into it. About ten days later I received a letter from him saying that the matter had been investigated and there was absolutely no evidence that Mr. "K" was a subversive. Tragically, the letter was unsigned. The ambassador had been killed in a crash at the Ottawa airport the day after the letter was written, and his secretary had sent it along to me without a signature.

Arthur Irwin became the new Film Board Commissioner. He had been publisher of *Maclean's* and his wife, Pat, a poet and artist, had worked in the film-strip division of the Film Board. When Arthur and the board decided to move operations to Montreal, many of us felt it was a mistake. The ambience for French and English writers, artists, and musicians, had been provided by the National Film Board in our bicultural national capital. We were losing that focus, and on a more selfish note, we were also losing many of our musicians from the Ottawa Philharmonic Orchestra when they went to Montreal with the Film Board.

John Grierson and company were the real pioneers of Canadian films. To many of us looking back, despite the highs of their endeavours and the lows of the bad moments, on balance they "built better than they knew," to Canada's great benefit.

My interest in theatre really began at McGill, where I was active in the Red and White Revues and the University Players' Workshop. I must say, that my interest was infinitely greater than my talent, at least as an actor, and I soon found that I could contribute best to the organizational side of things.

These early involvements, and having seen a lot of theatre, good and not so good, in New York and London over the years, led to a keen interest in the Little Theatre movement. I became a member of the executive as national treasurer of the Dominion

Drama Festival from 1952 to 1955. Dick MacDonald, the DDF's Executive Director, created a sound foundation in our country for the training of actors and directors and helped many audiences become more knowledgeable and appreciative of the good things to come. For me, the theatre was like a doorway that opened to exciting experiences. Fortunately, I could participate in adventures of major theatrical importance to Canada: Stratford and the National Arts Centre.

The Stratford experience began for me one day when my secretary told me that a Mr. Tom Patterson, from Stratford, Ontario, would like to see me. I knew about Tom, of course. Who didn't? That day, like most, Tom looked small in an ill-fitting suit a size or two too large for him. He didn't bother with any amenities but immediately introduced his subject – the Stratford dream. In a few moments Tom had convinced me.

The Stratford dream was Tom's dream. He started with a magical name, Stratford, and built from that to the concept of a great Shakespearean theatre in that small Ontario town, which, in 1953, was a tired railway junction point with a sleepy main business section.

Tom sold the idea and, in February of 1953, a starting goal of $150,000 was set. He expected to raise $30,000 in Stratford itself, although townspeople told him that Stratford had never raised more than $25,000, and that for a wartime charity. Nevertheless, in ten days they raised $42,000. With this beginning, Tom believed that the rest of the country would follow, and the objective of $150,000 could be raised easily. He was wrong, but he was not discouraged that it took three months to raise $5,000 from the rest of Canada. By that time contracts had been signed with Tony Guthrie, Alec Guinness, Tanya Moiseiwitsch, Cecil Clarke, and several others. Thousands of dollars were owing to the contractor, Oliver Gaffney, who was preparing the huge tent theatre. This debt, Tom says, did not stop Mr. Gaffney from working his regular twenty-four hour shift.

The only answer was another Stratford campaign. It proceeded with wide support. Another $30,000 was raised, but $25,000 of that was contributed by the Perth Mutual Insurance Company. Tom remembers that Stratford, at this point, had supplied almost half of the money. He maintains that they have

128

never really received credit for this. All of us who have been associated with the theatre know he is right. We know, too, of the energy and inspiration that flowed from Tom through the town to the average household. The people of Stratford opened their homes, welcomed guests, and even babysat with the children of theatre-goers, including our son, when he was too young for the evening performances in the early days.

Eventually, Tom and the committee had their $150,000. With this amount, plus the revenue from the box office, they could pay for the tent theatre, the "star English contingent" (Tom's words), the company of sixty-four Canadian actors, and the mounting of two major productions. A six-week season was launched. Artistically, it was the greatest theatrical moment Canada had ever known.

The other great inspiration of the Stratford miracle was Tyrone Guthrie. I asked Tom to tell me about Guthrie's first visit to Stratford when they drove from Toronto. Tom recalls that he was more and more anxious as they came closer to the town. Trying to make Tony's first impression a good one, he turned off Ontario Street to go down by the river. Even that was pretty dreary because the river had been drained, and all they saw was a sea of mud, with a few trickles of water running through it. Undeterred, Tom pointed out the piece of land he thought would be the most suitable for the permanent theatre–the present site. Tony agreed but wanted to look further. After Tom had parked the car on the drive directly below where the theatre now stands, Tony walked over to the island. It was early May, and the spring cleanup had not yet taken place.

Oblivious to the litter, Tony suggested to Tom with his usual gusto, "Why don't we do the whole thing in large barges? We could have each scene set up on a barge. It could play near the bridge to the island and then disappear around behind for changes to the next scene. The audience would be in bleachers over here," he said, pointing to the present parking lot. And then he suddenly rejected the whole idea in almost the same sentence, announcing, "Sorry, I don't think it will work."

Most people who knew Guthrie would agree with Tom when he says: "One of the most exciting things about Guthrie was his capacity for not dismissing any idea until he had thoroughly gone through it. Then, without any recriminations, he could drop it and go on to the next with the same enthusiasm. He could do this whether the idea was his or somebody else's."

As for my small part at this juncture, Tom arranged a meeting with Monte Monteith, the Member of Parliament from Stratford, so that Monte, his wife Mary, Audrey, and I could make a list of all the people in Ottawa who might be interested in the Stratford theatre. They came to cocktails at our house to hear the first chairman of the board, Dr. Showalter, when he came to Ottawa with Tom, to make the "pitch" for money. We raised some money, but more important, we formed a nucleus of Ottawa supporters and friends of Stratford who were steadfast over all the years.

The first funding objective for the new theatre was $550,000. The money was raised but the actual cost finally came to over $2,000,000 without air-conditioning. A few years later, when we added the air-conditioning, the total investment had risen to $2,250,000. We thought it was so much then, but considering our present inflated dollar, it is amazing that this noble theatre, certainly one of the great theatres of its kind in the world, could have been built for such a small amount.

Having been an avid supporter of Stratford from the early beginnings, I was troubled one spring to learn that *The Merchant of Venice* was scheduled for production that season. After considering the matter for a time, I decided to write a letter to the theatre board in the knowledge that the production would go on as scheduled, in any event. My main point was that while *Merchant* was unquestionably one of Shakespeare's great masterpieces, there could be equally no question that Shylock, properly portrayed, was a portrait and prototype for anti-Semitic caricature all the way through history to *Der Stürmer*. I stated that I could certainly see no objection to the staging of *Merchant* at some later time, after the company had presented most of the other outstanding plays in the bard's portfolio, but that to do so at this early stage seemed to me to create a real risk of offending many patrons, Jewish and non-Jewish alike. I further stated that the letter was entirely a private expression and that I had no intention of creating a *cause célèbre* but that I did feel it only fair and responsible to make my views known to the Board.

A short time later, I was contacted by Alfred Bell, who was Chairman of the Board at that time. He was visiting Ottawa, and called me from the home of my friend Adelaide Sinclair, then a member of the Board of Stratford. Alfred asked if he could come to see me. We had a brief discussion about the future of the Stratford theatre, and later I was invited to join the Board. I was pleased and flattered to become involved at that exciting time. Michael Langham had just arrived and Tony Guthrie was leaving. Tony had decided to leave because "his theatre was built," "his" stage, designed with Tanya Moiseiwitsch, was there, and the theatre was an enormous artistic success. He believed that a theatre should have new life frequently, and only new directors could provide that. Concerned that Stratford would become "Guthrie's theatre," and believing that Michael would be a fine successor, Tony left Stratford.

Tony Guthrie was a great man in every way. His ideas soared to creative heights, but he realized that he, like Icarus, might fly too close to the sun. His control held the performance and kept it from melting.

Many people of the theatre preferred to take a small part in a play directed by Guthrie than an important part in a play directed by someone else. His talent as a director transcended the theatre and extended to producing contemporary operas at the Metropolitan. As Rudolph Bing wrote: "The one complete success we had with a modern opera was the revival of *Peter Grimes*, in which the direction of Tyrone Guthrie and the conducting of Colin Davis combined to convince even our more skeptical subscribers that they were in attendance at a great performance of a wonderful opera."[*]

Michael Langham brought to Stratford a boundless enthusiasm, which was quiet and controlled. He had an eye not only for the beautiful, but also for the particular grace of theatre, the small but exquisite nuances and lightness that bring magic from the very dramatic. Some people believed that Michael's explanations of performances were the best shows in town. He took as long as two hours to discuss the plays, explaining what he believed Shakespeare really meant.

[*] *The Memoirs of Sir Rudolph Bing: 5000 Nights at the Opera* (New York: Popular Library, 1972), p. 211.

131

These were full years at Stratford, with many triumphs: *Twelfth Night, A Midsummer Night's Dream, Henry V. Hamlet* was superb, with Christopher Plummer, and there were so many other memorable moments. There was also the excitement of the beginning of opera at Stratford, with Benjamin Britten's *The Rape of Lucretia* with Regina Resnick. She called one day to ask which night we would arrive to see Lucretia raped; the rape occurred nightly at 10:10 P.M., she said. We were there the following week to see a pretty special rape with Jon Vickers as raper and Regina as rapee. After the performance, the "ravished maiden" prepared a most wonderful supper at the house she was renting. She was assisted by her stage attacker, and they sang duets from whatever opera came into their heads. She proudly showed the company her beautiful black and blue bruises—evidence of Jon's aggressiveness in the rape scene.

The emergence of fine actors from Stratford is one of its greatest gifts to the nation. I remember so well, in the early years of the festival, sitting on the verandah of our boarding-house when a young actor walked up and joined me. He asked whether I liked the performance of the former evening. It was Bill Hutt, who would emerge as a fine actor-director, one who did not heed the blandishments of the American stage or movies, but stayed on at Stratford. To some of us he has had rewards far greater than the material ones of some of his former colleagues, the respect of his peers as a fine performer, the admiration of the Canadian public, and the highest award the Government of Canada can bestow—Companion of the Order of Canada.

What a galaxy of artistic splendour has flourished at Stratford: John Colicos, Christopher Plummer, Kate Reid, Frances Hyland, the late Leo Ciceri, Mervyn Blake, Eric Christmas, Tony van Bridge, Douglas Campbell, Bernard Behrens, Pat Galloway, Jack Creley, William Needles, Peter Donat, Bruno Gerussi, Amelia Hall, Max Helpmann, Toby Robins, Ann Casson, Diana Maddox, Martha Henry, among many others.

In 1967, for many of the same reasons Tony Guthrie had left, Michael Langham decided that it was time to go. He too felt that there must be a new and invigorating climate created and that could come only with a new director. We regretted that Michael was leaving us, but we recognized the validity of his position.

132

Faced with the prospect of the appointment of a new artistic director, it was not unnatural for the Board to wish to appoint a Canadian. Accordingly, Jean Gascon was appointed the same year Michael Langham left. The new director brought to Stratford a deep and thorough knowledge of theatre. He had formed, almost single-handedly, one of Canada's most successful, imaginative and exciting theatres, Le Théâtre du Nouveau Monde, in Montreal. Jean is endowed with an innate sense of theatre and an ability to achieve the best in it. He loved the "business" of the stage – all the small, well-timed moments that produce a laugh or a sigh.

During these years there developed an attitude about engaging actors of great stature who were not Canadian. I disagreed with this because I believe that a great performance by an exceptionally fine actor makes for a higher quality performance by all the actors in the play. We were becoming "self-consciously" Canadian at a time when the maturity that Stratford had reached should have transcended this rather provincial attitude. It would be nonsense to bar Nureyev from dancing with the Canadian Ballet because he was originally from the Soviet. But that was the prevailing feeling for a time, and I think Stratford suffered as a result. Another reason for this somewhat "duller" period at Stratford had to do with the attitudes that were developing on the Board itself. It was thought important that new appointments to the Board be men of solid business stature, because Stratford had indeed become "big business." But it was also important that there be understanding and appreciation of theatre. In the latter years, particularly, I felt that a "big-business" attitude dominated, and too often the dollar-versus-taste battle was joined.

Although the specific reasons were never discussed directly, I hope that I was asked to join the Board because I could bring a combination of business experience and a "sense and love of theatre" that I felt would be beneficial in some way to the concept of Stratford.

Max Meighen, my friend over all of the years since high school, was on the Board and introduced me at my first Board meeting. His introduction was amusing, and a short time ago, with some friends at dinner, he recalled with a smile: "I remem-

133

ber well your first meeting as a director of the Board of the Stratford Shakespearean Festival. With a serious mien I advised the Board that we were very fortunate to have, at last, a director with artistic experience. I told them: 'I present to you the program director, the chief actor, singer, and dancer of the Red and White Revue, McGill University, 1929—Mr. Lawrence Freiman.'"

Other members of the Board brought fine combinations of talents and a knowledge and understanding of the theatre. They included Robertson Davies, Floyd Chalmers, George Harris. But there was one who, more than anyone, brought a love and affection to the theatre and all of the people associated with it. The lady, of course, was Dama Bell. She made not only an immense contribution to the Board, but became for everyone the "house mother" of Stratford. From the beginning, the dedication of Alfred and Dama Bell has been essential to Stratford's well being. Alfred Bell's contribution during his chairmanship, and over the many years he served on the Board, was inspirational. Alfred and Dama seemed to run a constant "open house," which lasted from opening night until the end of the season. At a party at their house there would be long chats with Tanya Moiseiwitsch, Brian Jackson, Desmond Healey, Robert Prévost, or any of the other renowned designers of Stratford.

There would often be parties in the Green Room of the theatre or an after-theatre drink and later to my friend the late Mr. Lee's Chinese restaurant, The Golden Dragon, for egg rolls, chicken sweet and sour, or one of his mysterious specialities. There might be a moment with Kate Reid when one would be almost overwhelmed with her *joie de vivre*, and the waves of excitement she made you feel when she discussed a particular play. I met Kate at a party in the Green Room when she first came to Stratford. To make cocktail party "chatter," I made some inane comment about finally meeting her and that I had a particular advantage. The advantage, I told her, stemmed from the fact that I felt I knew her because I had seen her frequently on television. Of course, she did not know me at all. Kate countered by saying that this was one of the rudest remarks she had ever heard. More than a little startled, I asked her why. She informed me that when she had been appearing in Ottawa a year or two before, Audrey and I had asked her and some of the other players to our home for cocktails!

No account of Stratford could be complete without a word about my friend, Mr. Smith, who was never John or Jim, but always Mr. Smith, and who, with his wife, ran the Imperial Motel, which was one of the first to open long before the "grand" ones. From the beginning, Mr. Smith looked after my wife and me and our friends very well. Nicholas Monsarrat would be at the motel as well as Rob Davies, and his delightful wife Brenda, and other of our friends.

For some years Nicholas had been the other Ottawa member of the Board and we made our "journeys" to the Board meetings together. We had tried every form of transportation, including the train which left Ottawa at midnight on Friday and arrived in Toronto at 7:00 A.M., leaving for Stratford forty minutes later. That train would get us into Stratford just in time for our 11:00 meeting on Saturday morning. This, of course, was an unpleasant way to go, and we finally resolved our problem in a most elegant manner. Anyone who knows Nicholas knows that only the really elegant appeals to him. We decided to take an 8:30 A.M. plane to Toronto, have a large car and chauffeur meet us at the airport, and drive to Stratford, where the chauffeur would stay all day until we returned to Malton airport, sometimes not until 12:30 or so the following morning. But we did have a good time, although Nicholas accused me of "never running out of words." I would then reciprocate in kind with a dubious compliment. The basic difference was that Nicholas spoke as impeccably as he wrote, and listening to him (when I gave myself the opportunity) was as enjoyable as reading one of his books.

It might be a good thing not to awaken fully from Tom Patterson's "dream," but to retain the enchantment and fantasy so that Stratford can continue as a physical reality and as a world of make-believe.

As I took my children when they were young, my daughter will take her children this season. And so the beauty of the great bard's plays is passed on, as it should be, from generation to generation. My years of association with the Stratford theatre were years of enchantment.

The National Capital

My years on the Federal District Commission (now the National Capital Commission) were notable in large part because of the distinction of my colleagues, including the late Dr. Charles Camsell, and Dr. B.K. Sandwell, the celebrated journalist and publisher of *Saturday Night*. Our duties were made fascinating by the skills of chairmen Senator Duncan McTavish and, subsequently, General Howard Kennedy. A quiet responsibility was brought to our discussions by the knowledgeable and not-easily-deterred Alan Hay, general manager of the commission. The nearly eight years in which I had the honour to serve on the commission would alone provide enough material for a book, but I will mention only a few of the highlights of that exciting period.

The commission had the good fortune to have as its consultant Jacques Gréber, who had been appointed by Prime Minister King. His inspiration touched the lives of so very many people, and, in fact, the very life of the national capital. He had more to do with its development than anyone.

Jacques Gréber, who came from Paris, was a smallish, elegant man with light blue, sparkling eyes. He could speak with equal knowledge of architecture, design, town planning or, in a lighter mood, of gourmet cooking and splendid wines. He feared contemporary architecture because he recognized the need in it for complete purity of line. He believed that solid buildings of high quality were essential for the capital.

It was M. Gréber who conceived the Green Belt for the national capital region – undoubtedly, his greatest contribution. With complete enthusiasm, the commission recommended his Green Belt plan to the interparliamentary committee responsible for considering matters that were deemed of vital importance. The Green Belt would be precisely what the name implies – an area of green encircling the national capital – requiring that development be restricted to the area inside the belt. It would preclude the possibility of unplanned and unco-ordinated development resulting in the disorder of sprawl. It would allow for orderly development of services, housing, and schools, all well-planned and dotted with broad open spaces and parks. It would provide a significant base for a great national capital of the future. The government agreed, and the Green Belt was begun.

136

Recently, the former Chairman of the National Capital Commission, the eminent Edgar Gallant, agreed that the Green Belt was one of the three most vital elements in the successful future planning of the national capital. The two others of vital importance were Gatineau Park and the development of the highway system on rights-of-way acquired from the railways. Here, too, Jacques Gréber made his presence felt.

It is a remarkable gift to be able to resolve simply the most complicated situations. Jacques Gréber possessed this gift in abundance. Historically, Ottawa's growth had been shaped largely by the many railroad lines criss-crossing from the pulp and paper mills in Hull. To most of us, the rail lines were a chaotic eyesore. To M. Gréber, they represented rare good fortune. He explained that it would be a simple process to deal with only two companies, the CNR and the CPR, to take over the lines required.

"We can take over the lines," he said, "and convert them to arterial highways from nearly all surrounding points, all connecting to the centre of the city." This is basically what we did. Here was a tremendous wheel, the spokes of which ran to the centre core with few intersections. There is no doubt that this simple plan helped immensely to re-vitalize downtown Ottawa.

M. Gréber's approach to Gatineau Park was equally simple. He believed passionately that the Gatineau provided an exquisite backdrop for the national capital and feared that if something was not done to protect it, its hills would be denuded, commercial signs would mar its beauty, and unstructured, sprawling development would forever contaminate this magnificent setting.

With his usual eloquence, M. Gréber stated his case to the commission. We asked what could be done to protect the area. His answer was typically direct. "Well, of course, you just buy it," he shrugged. This is exactly what we did. Even before I left the commission, we had purchased around 55,000 of the estimated 100,000 acres needed for the park. The beautiful scenic drives were planned and begun. When complete, these unique drives will proceed along the tops of the hills by Meach Lake to Lac LaPeche, and back to Hull on the east side of the hills, opening up incredible new vistas to thousands of people.

One evening over cocktails I said to Doug Fullerton, who was then Chairman of the National Capital Commission, that my participation in the decision to purchase the land for Gatineau Park was probably one of the most significant recommendations in which I had ever been involved. Doug agreed that probably nothing will affect the national capital in the next 100 years as will maintaining the beauty of this remarkable woodland.

There were many other gratifying activities in those days. We were buying land for the Ottawa River Parkway, which has turned out to be practical and beautiful, and we were involved in purchasing the land and planning the Queensway, which would change the socio-economic life of the national capital. These plans were of tremendous magnitude and expense, and they rank among the most advanced and imaginative steps in urban planning in North America.

We placed a well-designed city hall in a beautiful setting at Green's Island. It is a memorial for a fine Canadian architect, who was also my friend, Vincent Rother of Montreal. In a way, too, it is a memorial to Ottawa's "fightin' Mayor," my dear friend and former colleague on the commission, the late Charlotte Whitton. It was under her administration that a contest of architects was held, the Royal Canadian Architectural Institute adjudicating the designs submitted. I think Charlotte was not too pleased with the design chosen, a view shared by our Chairman, General Kennedy. But to their credit, the city hall was built, and is one in which the city can take pride.

Those days also saw the development of Sussex Drive into a ceremonial avenue for great national occasions. Adding to its dignity and charm are the many old buildings that have been beautifully restored to maintain their over-century-old character, blending attractively with the striking contemporary design of the Lester Pearson Building, Canada's Building for External Affairs. Further along the Drive are the lush green rolling lawns that have replaced the dilapidated houses that once stood there, then the External Affairs, the French Embassy, the South African Embassy, the Prime Minister's residence, and eventually Rideau Hall, residence of the Governor General. Many heads of state have driven down Sussex Drive in this past decade and there is satisfaction in knowing that I participated, in my years with the Federal District Commission, in the planning of this prestigious roadway. When completed, Sussex Drive will be one of the most significant ceremonial avenues in any nation's capital.

I had been appointed to the commission by Prime Minister St. Laurent originally for a term of five years. On an extremely busy night just before Christmas, I was in the toy department of the store, surrounded by countless children and customers, when I was called to the telephone. It was shortly after 8:00 in the evening, and the voice at the other end of the line said, "Is this Mr. Freiman? This is Louis St. Laurent speaking. I am trying to clear up my desk," he said, "as I am leaving tomorrow on a vacation my doctor tells me I require. Before leaving, it is important for me to know whether you would accept another appointment to the Federal District Commission, as it is my desire to reappoint you."

I was flattered that the Prime Minister, in his over-busy day, had found time for such a call. In those days, the Prime Minister was also the minister responsible for the Federal District Commission, and Mr. St. Laurent, like his predecessors, took a keen interest in the development of the national capital. He complimented me on my contribution to the commission, and I told him I would be pleased to accept another appointment for a three-year term.

Some months before that term was to expire, a government messenger arrived at my office with a large, carefully bound package. Opening it, I was surprised to see that it was a huge scroll with the seal of Canada embossed on it. The wording stated that I had been appointed a member of the Federal District Commission. The date went back over two-and-a-half years. I was even more surprised a few days later at the Press Club Ball, when friends chided me about the CBC report that afternoon which had said that, along with eighteen others, I had been "removed" from the commission. In other words, I was one of the nineteen out of twenty members who had been "fired." The Conservatives had won the recent election and Mr. Diefenbaker had obviously decided that a Liberal-appointed commission simply "wouldn't do." The one member of the commission not removed was the gifted Sandy Walker of Vancouver, who was extremely ill when the list of "removals" was announced, and to have included him would not have been politic. Having known Mr. Diefenbaker for many years, I am confident that there was nothing personal in his decision and that it was probably natural for him to think in party terms. But at the same time, I don't think most of us had considered our appointments as being political. In any event, my years with the commission were gratifying and intensely interesting, and I know that we were all proud and grateful for the opportunity to help develop the National Capital.

Social Development
On the Rideau River Parkway beside Tunney's Pasture, near the Department of Health and Welfare Building, stands another "house"–one we began to build under the chairmanship of Brigadier General Preston Gilbride, when I was President of the Canadian Welfare Council, now the Canadian Council on Social Development. In the days of my youth, the council had been housed in a small residence around the corner from our home on Somerset Street. Charlotte Whitton was Executive Director of Child Welfare then, and as the work expanded she became Director of the Welfare Council. As social welfare needs grew during the Depression years, so did the need for larger quarters.

During the more than twenty-five years that I served on the council, there were many opportunities to work for change, much of it inspired by directors George Davidson* and his successor Dick Davis. More than any other man, George Davidson helped me to realize that an individual can influence policy and contribute to productive change without running for Parliament, the provincial legislature, or the city council. What we achieved is evident in the records of the council. Dick Davis described the council as a national association of public and private agencies and of individuals concerned with the advancement of social welfare and its essential services.

Four areas of social legislation had particular interest for me during my years on the council. With the recession of the early

*Deputy Minister of Health and Welfare. After serving as Secretary of the Treasury Board, he went on to become President of the CBC and then to serve as a Deputy Director General of the United Nations.

1950s, unemployment became an acute problem. Many unemployed workers were either not covered by unemployment insurance or had exhausted their benefits. The only remaining source of help was private charity.

Proposals had come from the National Employment Commission in 1938, the Sirois Commission in 1941, and the federal government in proposals to the provinces in 1945. These proposals were designed to establish a special provincial unemployment assistance program that would be in addition to the unemployment insurance fund financed and administered by the federal government. The council opposed the plan, believing that it was neither sound in principle nor workable in practice. Traditionally, public assistance had been a provincial responsibility; two national systems, one provided by the federal government and one by the provinces, would involve costly administrative duplication, and endless disputes over which jurisdiction would be responsible for a person in need. The council's alternative was to broaden existing provincial and municipal assistance programs to cover, in addition to unemployables, the employable unemployed. We recommended that the federal authority, consistent with its 1945 proposals, would cover the cost of assistance and services to the provinces and municipalities. It would be, in practice, a partnership of the various levels of government. Administrative responsibility would remain with the provinces, but federal funding would be held in reserve to prevent any repetition of the municipal bankruptcies and over-burdened provincial budgets that had occurred during the Depression. In the council's view, it was this experience of the 1930s that had caused provinces and municipalities to limit their responsibility to the care of unemployables. The council's views were presented to the federal government in March 1953. No action was taken. In early 1955, as council President, I led another small delegation to meet with the Cabinet.

We decided to emphasize the obligation of governments to come together in a conference to work out a mutually satisfactory plan. We adopted this objective, rather than arguing for our own proposals, because we felt it would be more acceptable to the Cabinet. C.D. Howe, Acting Prime Minister in the absence of Mr. St. Laurent, chaired the meeting.

"Ridiculous," snorted Mr. Howe, when he had heard the opening statement. "For us to call such a conference would be tantamount to accepting the responsibility in what is clearly a provincial field, and that we cannot and will not do."

I asked him whether there would be any objection to the council calling a conference. "Not at all," he replied. "The council can do what it pleases."

The delegation proceeded to the Chateau Laurier, set a date, and booked the necessary rooms. That same afternoon, telegrams were dispatched to the provincial premiers and the Prime Minister, inviting them to a conference under the council's auspices. It was an audacious move. Soon, replies were received from various provinces agreeing to be represented. But the federal government held back. I was informed that two letters had been drafted by senior officials, but neither was acceptable to the Prime Minister.

A short time later, I received a telephone call from the Prime Minister, inviting me to visit him to discuss the matter. The appointment was made for that same day. The substance of the interview was that it was awkward for the federal government to be officially represented at a conference called by a private agency, but to decline the invitation might be construed as indifference to a pressing social problem. The Prime Minister suggested that he call a meeting of provincial premiers. This conference would not be specifically on unemployment, but would consider the matter if it were brought up. Would the council, under these circumstances, cancel its conference? I replied that it would.

This federal-provincial conference was held on April 27-29, 1955, and shortly thereafter a joint federal-provincial program of assistance came into being. The conference and resulting program revised the unemployment assistance program in three ways: first, it filled a serious and long-standing gap in income maintenance provision; second, it was to be administered by the provinces; third, it eliminated the difficulties in distinguishing between employable and unemployable persons in need. It also provided the foundations for the Canada Assistance Plan which became effective a decade later.

The second area of social legislation that I found especially important was rehabilitation of disabled Canadians. No one denied that if a Canadian soldier lost a leg on the battlefield the government had a responsibility for his welfare. But what about the civilian who lost a leg in an automobile accident? Encouraged by the success of the rehabilitation program for veterans after the Second World War, the council and a number of its affiliated national health organizations tackled the job of getting that same assistance extended to civilians. After several unsuccessful attempts to interest senior officials of the Department of Labour, the council arranged a meeting with the minister, Humphrey Mitchell, in early 1950. He expressed an unexpected interest. We immediately struck a committee to formulate a program that would combine medical aid, vocational training, and special employment placement services. Next, a national conference on the Rehabilitation of Handicapped Civilians was convened in Toronto by the Ministers of Labour, Health and Welfare, and Veteran Affairs. The conference established a National Advisory Committee and a national co-ordinator was appointed in January 1953. That spring, Parliament appropriated additional funds for a new program that included the appointment of provincial co-ordinators and the maintenance of their offices and organizations; a rehabilitation grant under the National Health Grants program; and the Vocational Training program for additional and special courses.

Undoubtedly, because of my close involvement with Mother's and Father's untiring efforts on behalf of immigrants, the whole area of immigration interested me deeply. The history of Canadian immigration policy, especially through the twenties and thirties and beyond is one of the most inglorious periods in the life of this nation. It could so easily have been a noble page in our record. Even after the war, when over two million immigrants came to Canada between 1956 and 1960, the problems were legion. The most serious included reception, including accommodation and assistance on arrival, protection under social security measures. Immigrants were not entitled to receive family allowance until they had been in Canada one year, nor were they entitled to unemployment insurance until they could qualify after making regular payments. Further there was a deportation clause, which provided that under certain circumstances an immigrant could be deported if he had received public assistance.

In 1954, after having made no headway against getting these discriminatory rules changed, the council appointed yet another committee on the welfare of immigrants. Chaired by my brother-in-law, Bernard Alexandor, the committee was made up of representatives from national and local organizations, interested individuals, and "observers" from appropriate federal departments and certain embassies. The committee held its first meeting in Ottawa on December 7, 1954, and appointed subcommittees to study two important items of wide concern: the eligibility of immigrant children for family allowance, and the immigration act clause concerning the deportation of people who became public charges.

By the spring of 1956 we had made some progress. Parliament approved a recommendation of the Minister of Citizenship and Immigration that each immigrant or settler be paid $60 a year for each child under sixteen years of age during the first year when family allowance is not paid. The council's recommendation that the federal government repeal the deportation clause was not acted on.

But the pressure on government continued. Representatives of the council, under Mr. Alexandor's leadership, met again with officials of the Departments of Citizenship and Immigration, National Health and Welfare, and Labour to discuss a council memorandum on unemployment assistance for immigrants. This memorandum, which set forth alternative methods of giving assistance to unemployed "new Canadians" during their first year here, was well received. The delegation received assurance that improvements would be made in the methods by which emergency assistance is provided to newcomers. Shortly after, at the request of the Department of Citizenship and Immigration, representatives of the Committee on the Welfare of Immigrants met with officials to advise on rates for unemployed immigrants. To a substantial degree the council's recommendations were accepted and put into effect.

Despite the frustrations, the council persevered in its efforts to have other inequities removed. It appointed a sub-committee in October 1958, under the chairmanship of Dr. Eugene Forsey, to study the Immigration Act with a view to revision. It also initiated correspondence with the federal and provincial governments regarding hospital insurance protection for immigrants and others of non-resident status.

The meetings continued and are continuing, but the existing inequities in our immigration policies testify to how little meaningful progress has been made over the years.

There is still a great need for better regulations and better legislation. The history of immigration in our country is not a history in which Canadians can take pride, nor is it worthy of the principles in which most Canadians believe.

The fourth area of great concern to me, and to many members of the council, was the question of capital punishment. Some of us believed that the death penalty did not serve as a deterrent to murder. Instead of fitting the mores of a civilized society, it relegated us to the medieval.

As early as 1953, during my presidency, the annual meeting of the Delinquency and Crime Division of the council adopted a resolution calling for the immediate abolition of capital punishment. The resolution was to be forwarded to the Joint Parliamentary Committee on Corporal and Capital Punishment and Lotteries. But divided opinion within the council, as to the appropriate timing, delayed action for two years. Then, in 1955, after some revision, the resolution was presented to the Joint Parliamentary Committee as official council policy. At the same time, the brief was circulated to a number of organizations in the fields of corrections, education, law, business, and labour, inviting their support. Press comment was extensive and ranged from high praise to condemnation.

After thirty meetings the parliamentary committee recommended retention of the death penalty, although it also recommended that capital punishment be subjected to periodic review by Parliament. Yet, as a constructive contribution to public understanding, a desire to explore the conscience of Canadians, and as an attempt to awaken the disinterested spirit on a question of immense moral consequence concerning life and death itself, the efforts of the council were vital. In time, of course, the efforts paid off. On June 21, 1976, the House of Commons voted, by a narrow margin, to abolish the death penalty in Canada.

On June 15, in one of the most eloquent speeches of his

career, Prime Minister Trudeau, urging the Commons to abolish the death penalty, said, in part:

> Are we, as a society, so lacking in respect for ourselves, so lacking in hope for human betterment, so socially bankrupt that we are ready to accept state vengeance as our penal philosophy? My primary concern here is not compassion for the murderer. My concern is for the society which adopts vengeance as an acceptable motive for its collective behaviour. If we make that choice, we will snuff out some of that boundless hope and confidence in ourselves and other people, which has marked our maturing as a free people. We will have chosen violence as a weapon against the violence we profess to abhor.

It took all those years for this civilized nation to reach this conclusion.

Of my various involvements, my work with the council was the most frustrating. Everything seemed to take so long, and the needs were real and pressing. Yet, in retrospect, it was worth it, for despite the endless hours of sometimes aimless debate, and the months of seemingly unnecessary delays, the council did contribute to a better quality of life.

Bicultural Learning
In the fall of 1946 a small delegation led by Mr. Lucien Massé came to see me on behalf of the University of Ottawa. The delegation was raising funds for a medical school, to be built by the university. They presented a splendid case for the serious need in Ottawa for a medical school. Assuring the delegation that I would contribute funds to the project, I asked one question, which seemed rather obvious but apparently had not yet been asked. It was whether the medical school would be open to all qualified candidates, irrespective of race, creed, or colour. Operated by the Oblate Fathers at that time, it was a Roman Catholic, bilingual university. I assured the delegation that I would contribute to the medical school whether it was restricted to Roman Catholic students or not, but I hoped that they would adopt the principle of a school open to all candidates. Mr. Massé was most

sympathetic to my question and told me he would take it up with the Chancellor of the university, Archbishop Alexandre Vachon, and return to inform me of the decision.

Archbishop Vachon was a scientist, a patrician of intelligence, and sensitivity. When Mr. Massé relayed the question to him, he replied, "I would have expected no less of a question from Mr. Freiman. Please inform him that the criteria for admission to the university now and for all time, not only in the medical faculty but in all faculties, will be based on academic standards only." This principle actually had been enunciated as far back as 1848 by the founder of the university, Bishop Eugene Guigues, O.M.I. who said:

> Bytown will prove to be a most judicious site for the establishment of a college, since it is a growing town situated in the centre of an ever-increasing population. Indeed, the college will solidly cement the most durable bonds among the youth of different origins and faiths and will erase the natural antipathies always so deplorable (when they exist) among the citizens of a common country.

In 1946, Archbishop Vachon's statement was an important endorsement of a very important principle. Even at my own university, McGill, it was said there was a "quota" for Jewish students, and it was becoming more difficult for them to get into the professional faculties, particularly into the faculty of medicine. At the University of Ottawa the irony was that the school was Roman Catholic in fact, but the Oblate Fathers' magnanimity and liberality made living fact of the principle of a multi-denominational university.

I was invited to join the Board of Regents in 1959 and became Vice-Chairman in 1960. Lionel P. McGowan was Chairman. These were extremely happy days for me. The Fathers were splendid educators and administrators, and very understanding and kind to their Vice-Chairman. They brought a charm and quiet sophistication to each dinner, at which was reflected their knowledge of food and wine. Audrey also loved to go to the university because of the thoughtfulness and many small attentions showered on her by the good Fathers.

The university was small then. We had approximately 1,700

undergraduates and graduate students, virtually every one of them known personally by the Rector, Father Henri François LeGaré (now the Archbishop of MacLennan, North Alberta). He was earnest, dedicated, and an intellectual with a most delightful sense of humour. As the university continued to grow it created more pressure for space in its midtown location. On various occasions, alternative plans to relocate the university in an area just outside the city limits were examined and rejected. We felt sure that it was right to develop a great university in the intellectual core of the national capital, close to the National Gallery, the National Archives, the National Library, and to Parliament itself.

As the years went by, more and more properties were acquired and new buildings started to rise. By 1959, the campus included the arts building, a medical school, several buildings housing departments of science and engineering, and the administration building. During the next five years a new wing was added to the medical school, a science library and two residences were built, and construction began on the building that now houses the computer science department.

Each year my close friend Roger Seguin, who later served as Chairman of the university's Board of Governors, Rector LeGaré, and I made our annual trek to Toronto for the funds the university required. The Ministry of Education provided financial support for the faculties of medicine and science and engineering, which the Ontario government had asked the university to establish in 1945. Funds were needed to expand these faculties. We frequently asked for funding for other faculties but were always met with the answer that the university would have to reorganize first. Under provincial legislation, a denominational university could not receive the amounts that non-denominational universities received. As growth continued, it became increasingly clear that if the university was to improve its academic standards and increase its enrolment, much greater funding would be required.

The principle that had established the bilingual and bicultural nature of the university was vital. In the core of the national capital there had to be an institution of higher learning dedicated to the cultures of the two founding peoples of our country. With

148

the nature and purpose of the university in mind, I established a Living Chair in Canadian History in 1959, in the name of my father. Dr. Guy Frégault, the eminent French-Canadian historian, was to hold the Chair as head of the history department of the arts faculty. Invited by the Rector to say a few words at the presentation ceremony I said, in part:

> A real appreciation of this fine heritage is necessary if future Canadian generations are to develop with a vitality for the realization of a great destiny. In this appreciation will lie an even greater truth. In ratio to the development of the understandings of these two great strains, to that extent will there be a more profound understanding of all peoples that constitute Canadian society.

When Dr. Frégault delivered his first lecture at the inauguration of the Chair, he said:

> If there is a place in this country where the study of Canadian history ought to develop in terms of both expansion and excellence, it is here. For here can be found, on the one hand, an incomparable wealth of material to work on in the Public Archives of Canada and, on the other hand, institutions of higher learning where students can be given the methodological tools, the professional training, the basic information, and, above all, the intellectual stimuli that are so necessary for one who wishes to engage in this demanding but exhilarating adventure: a career of historical research. In other words, Ottawa is the place of opportunity for Canadian historians. It presents the student and the research worker with facilities that are available nowhere else in Canada to the same extent.

As the years passed, with ever-increasing budget demands, the Fathers, supported by the Board of Regents, decided to make a most magnanimous gesture. Knowing that if the university ceased to be denominational, the province would provide much greater funding for capital development and maintenance, they decided in 1965 to reorganize the university corporation in order to qualify for full provincial support.

The assets were evaluated by a committee under the chairmanship of General Jean Victor Allard. After a series of meetings between the university and the province, the assets were subsequently transferred to the new university. Under the reorganization, the faculties of theology and canon law assumed the charter of the old University of Ottawa under the new name of Saint Paul University. That cleared the way for the rest of the university to be grouped under a new charter, using the old name, and to qualify for this new financial support from the province.

Under provincial legislation there were seven categories of appointment or election to the Board of Governors, one being by the university itself. I was one of the twelve chosen by the university to serve on its Board. When Chief Justice Fauteux was elected Chairman of the Board at its first meeting, he nominated me as Vice-Chairman. Shortly thereafter the Chief Justice retired, believing that as Chief Justice he could not be party to any suggestion of requesting funds for the university from the province. It was a source of regret to the Board, and certainly to me, that this great Canadian was not to lead us into this important phase of development. He did consent to be an honorary member of the Board and informed us that we would be able to call on him for advice and consultation.

A new era at the university had begun. It was expanding tremendously, both in student population and in academic standing, under the brilliant leadership of its Rector, Father Roger Guindon, and its two highly qualified Vice-Rectors, Dr. Maurice Chagnon, Vice-Rector, Academic, and Allan Gilmore, Vice-Rector, Administration.

General Jean Allard was elected Chairman, to be followed by Roger Seguin, and I continued as Vice-Chairman of the Board. Madame Vanier was appointed Chancellor, with the concurrence of the Senate, in 1966. It was not long before we found ourselves with a student population of close to 10,000 and a capital building program of approximately one hundred million dollars to meet the demand for more and more buildings in the area. Now we have the new Law Building, which was appropriately named Fauteux Hall, the magnificent Physical Education complex, the Library, the University Centre, a new building housing the engineering department, and two additional residences.

150

In a remarkably short time, we witnessed the development of a bicultural institution of higher learning in the national capital. It is hoped that the University of Ottawa will continue to respond to Toynbee's law of challenge, as described by Dr. Frégault at the presentation ceremony of the Freiman Living Chair in Canadian History: "It is difficult rather than easy conditions that produce the achievements by which a civilization is recognized as successful."

The National Arts Centre

This doorway was opened for me, fittingly enough, by a most distinguished man of letters, Vincent Massey, our first Canadian-born Governor General, who brought to his high office a "civilizing" influence and genuine love of the performing arts.

In a speech to the Ottawa Canadian Club in December 1952, he made an overwhelming impression on some of us about Ottawa's importance as a national capital. He presented a tremendous challenge, showing how we could attain Canadian cultural distinction in Ottawa. He said:

> And, while all Canadians are now proud of their capital, and while those who read the history of Bytown and visit the Ottawa of today are not only impressed by its functions and dignity and moved by its charm, there must still be a feeling that much more can happen here in the future. Ottawa is more than a pleasant and picturesque Canadian city. It is more than the site of parliament houses and government offices. It is more than the catering establishment for a vast number of more or less transient guests. It is the capital, and is becoming increasingly the centre of a nation with growing power and influence in this complicated world.

He then went on to suggest that there be an annual festival of music and arts, along the lines of the one held in Edinburgh. He believed it should be international in character, "but with a special emphasis on Canadian cultural achievement." It was prophetic of the Arts Centre when he said that such a festival "serves to promote those activities that know no barrier of language or of history or of politics; activities which demonstrate that distinction between mere escapism and distraction on the one hand and genuine recreation on the other; activities greatly needed in this difficult age." His Excellency proceeded to form a committee to discuss a national festival of the arts. The Chairman was Senator Duncan McTavish, assisted by the following members, of whom I was pleased to be one: Mrs. George Drew, Walter Herbert, Mrs. H.O. McCurry, Louis Audette, Paul Pelletier, Louis Rasminsky, H. Showalter, I. Norman Smith, and Robert Southam. As Honorary Chairman, the Governor General participated in the discussions. We were fortunate to receive his sincere interest, inspiration, and knowledge.

He invited to our meetings such distinguished gentlemen of the theatre and opera as Sir Rudolph Bing, Edward Johnson, Sir Tyrone Guthrie, and Ian Hunter. Each was so different from the other. Sir Rudolph Bing replied to all questions with implacable, cool, if not cold, logic. He was unsmiling, thorough, and sophisticated. Drawing from his experiences at Edinburgh, he argued for an international, rather than a strictly Canadian festival. He advised us that "the native arts, so to speak, will learn and grow by the impact of really outstanding foreign art with an older tradition and an older technique and background. They will grow by seeing it, and by measuring themselves against very stiff competition." Edward Johnson, with his blue, smiling eyes, white hair, and extreme good looks, brought charm, grace, and pleasure to the proceedings. He suggested that we try to find the money and then develop a plan. Tony Guthrie, on the other hand, insisted that the plan should come first. It should be grand on an international scale and should not over-emphasize things Canadian. He also felt that our idea of a one-week festival was "chickenhearted." With good humour, and conversational brilliance, he brought his love of anything theatrical to our discussions. Ian Hunter brought a practical, sound, business approach to the task of operating a festival.

The one important conclusion that came out of all our meetings was the need for a building in the national capital. Without a building there could not be a festival or, in fact, a proper setting for music and the performing arts generally.

This conclusion was reached after we realized that we could not depend on the summer weather, and that acoustics, lighting, and other technical requirements could not be met outside. The consensus was that these elements had to be professionally excellent. Tony Guthrie advised us against our proposed shell for musical performances with his usual perceptive optimism. He said, "You should make a plan which depends upon a building; and a pretty spectacular and sensational type of building."

Our Chairman, Senator McTavish, made informal representation to the government about a building, but to no avail.

In early 1963, fifty-five arts groups in the Ottawa region formed the National Capital Arts Alliance, under the guiding spirit of Hamilton Southam. This group was concerned with the lack of facilities for the performing arts in the national capital area. Some funds were raised privately to engage Dominion Consultants Associates of Montreal to prepare a report for the federal government. This report, known as the Brown Book, was presented to Prime Minister Pearson and the government in November 1963. It envisaged a national arts centre to "nurture and encourage growth and excellence in the performing arts among artists both in the national capital area and throughout Canada." The government approved. Hamilton Southam was seconded from the Department of External Affairs and appointed co-ordinator for the proposed centre.

There were many discussions and various suggestions on where the centre should be built. One Sunday morning in the fall of 1964, I received a telephone call from George McIlraith, now Senator McIlraith, who was then President of the Privy Council and Ottawa's representative in the Cabinet. Senator McIlraith, a fine parliamentarian, has given a life of service to Canada. He wanted Ottawa to become an important national capital and was mindful of the aesthetic requirements of that goal. The proposed arts centre, he believed, would play an important part. George is an old friend, and he was calling to ask my opinion on where the arts centre should be situated. "In front of Parliament," I replied. To my mind, it was the only site that could be or should be considered. The centre would be in front of Parliament, the adjacent buildings for the future might be the new National Gallery, and on the east of these buildings would be the University of Ottawa. I pointed out that if proper aesthetic consideration was given to these buildings and to the development of the university, there would be in the core of the city an intellectual and artistic presence in the national capital that would be inspirational to its future development. George said that these were the considerations that prompted his desire for the centre to be in its present location on Confederation Square.

It was good fortune that George McIlraith became the Cabinet minister responsible for the building, accepting the post of Minister of Public Works in 1965. During his ministry, while he "fought out" the problems of escalating costs, the building was substantially completed.

It was during this period too that Maurice Lamontagne, as Secretary of State, was contributing much to the development of cultural awareness throughout Canada. He created a climate for acceptance by the government, not only of the National Arts Centre, but also of the splendid cultural centre buildings in Charlottetown, Winnipeg, Saskatoon, Regina, and Victoria. He was the architect in the 1960s for the grand design for theatre, dance, and music of the seventies and the decades to follow. It was during his tenure as Secretary of State that one could see the transformation of what had been something of a "grab bag" department into what has become Canada's "department of culture."

As Canada's Centennial year approached, a Centennial committee was formed, and I was invited to be Chairman for the performing arts for the national capital. With the assistance of Freeman Tovell, Paul Pelletier, Bill Teron, Jack Nutter, Hamilton Southam, Louis Rasminsky, Yousuf Karsh, I. Norman Smith, Nicholas Goldschmidt, Mayor Marcel D'Amour of Hull, and Mayor Don Reid of Ottawa, we reinstituted the Canadian Festival of the Arts. Earl Crowe, the impresario, was our co-ordinator, and Jack Nutter was our efficient and untiring treasurer.

We invited Tony Guthrie to come to Ottawa to see what might be done to mark the Centennial in fitting ways. He visualized, facing the centre block of the Parliament Buildings, a large, temporary, circular structure that would seat an audience in the round. He visualized a theatrical legend of Canada beginning with Indian dances against a background of our mythic, Eden-like Canadian landscape. The legend would continue from the coming of the French and the English to the busy present day, and then take a fantasy-like look at the Canadian future. The central theme would be of the beauty and joy and fulfillment of our country. Tony believed that we had the Canadian designers, musicians, and writers who could create the artistic quality necessary for this significant occasion in Canadian history.

The Cabinet authorized an expenditure of $300,000, but after some months it was evident that this amount would not be nearly enough. The new amount looked like $750,000 and we could not be sure of staying within that figure. I was attending a Zionist conference in Geneva when I was contacted by Judy LaMarsh, who had become Secretary of State. She asked if we should cancel our plans, in view of the substantial increase in cost. I cabled agreement that we should, and our co-ordinator, Earl Crowe, was dispatched to New York to inform Sir Tyrone of the decision. He later informed me of Sir Tyrone's typically generous reply. He totally understood the situation and he expected no further fee in light of the circumstances. Although the idea of a grand spectacle was now dead, the performing arts section of the Centennial Commission, under the aegis of the Canadian Festival of the Arts, which we had set up for the purpose, did complete a most successful series during Centennial year. We staged over 100 performances, ranging from the New York Philharmonic, with Leonard Bernstein conducting, the International Film Festival of Laughter, and Les Feux Follets, to children's concerts, one of which was a very moving performance of *Noye's Fludde* by Benjamin Britten. This involved about 150 local children and was performed in Christ Church Cathedral and conducted by Nicholas Goldschmidt. It was one of the highlights of this exciting year.

It was basically because of the hard work and efficiency of Earl Crowe and his few dedicated colleagues that we achieved the highest attendance on record for a touring event in Canada. This was Festival Canada, the agency that took major attractions across Canada during the Centennial year. At the end of that year, we had not only done the job but were able to return $30,000 in government funds that had been allocated for the performing arts.

The evident success and the tremendous audiences that attended the Centennial events provided encouragement for the belief that, despite the reservations of some, there was a tremendous interest in the performing arts that would make the National Arts Centre the success that we believed it would be.

Early in 1966, during one of Tony Guthrie's visits to Ottawa when he stayed in our home, I invited the minister Judy LaMarsh to dinner to meet Tony so that we could discuss the Centennial project. As Tony, Judy, Audrey and I were having cocktails, Judy turned to me suddenly and asked, "How would you like to be Chairman of the National Arts Centre? The Prime Minister and I want you to do it. What do you say?" I was totally taken aback. Tony was startled, and Audrey, knowing of my many activities at this time, was crestfallen. I thanked Judy, said I would think it over, and would call her for an appointment at her convenience.

I was keenly sensitive to the continuing political outcry and the criticism of the media over the way building costs for the centre had escalated. My first concern was whether this atmos-phere would have a heavily negative impact on public acceptance of the centre. But the more I thought of it, the more clearly I saw that public fights over cost must not and would not detract from the rightness of the concept. It *was* a uniquely beautiful structure and the way to keep it that way was to make sure that it was the focal point of taste in the performing arts. The fact that a new face would emerge as Chairman, someone who had not been associated with the debate over building costs, might well help to diffuse the strident arguments that had surrounded the centre almost since it was started.

The next week, Judy and I met to discuss the following matters: (1) there was no question in my mind that the government would have to accept the substantial deficit that would be incurred by operating an arts centre of quality; (2) we were now in 1966, and the performing arts could no longer be funded by collecting money from individuals and corporations (it was impossible to try to raise from private sources the substantial amounts required to make the Arts Centre a success); (3) unless a substantial amount was funded by the government, I could not take the chairmanship. Judy asked what the amount would be. I told her that I did not know, but said I would try to arrive at reasonably accurate figures based on what I knew about the costs of symphonies and theatres generally and from my association

156

with the Ottawa Symphony and with Stratford. I invited her to ask the people in her department to develop figures at the same time so that we could compare the amounts required. We did this and came up with figures that were rather close. The total amount needed from government in the first year was two and a half million dollars. I believed that we could do a top quality job if we received these funds. After discussions of this amount with Hamilton Southam, he agreed.

It was to everyone's good fortune that Judy LaMarsh was the one who spoke for the Arts Centre in the House and in Cabinet. She was a splendid minister who fought tirelessly for the things she believed in–and she believed in the Arts Centre. After we agreed on the amount needed from the government, I asked Judy to have approval recorded in a minute of the Cabinet. She agreed and obtained Cabinet approval.

On that sunny, early autumn day in 1966, when I accepted the chairmanship, I walked down the steps of Parliament and stopped to look at the tremendous building that was emerging as our National Arts Centre. At that moment, I saw that not only did the new Chairman not have a secretary, he did not even have a typewriter at his disposal. Here was this great building emerging and the immediate need was for sound organization. The one thing I did have was my conviction that the Arts Centre would be a great success. If the centre was successful, it would encourage Canadian artists and would be a place where not only Canadians, but millions of tourists from the other nations of the world, would feel a great pride in Canada. But enough dreaming. The job was now to put together an organization that would make all of this happen.

I made countless organizational charts before Ernie Steele, the Under-Secretary of State at that time, and Henry Hindley, Assistant Under-Secretary of State, encouraged me to proceed with the simplest and most businesslike of them. From that point on, it was a matter of filling the slots with the right people. At the beginning, the inter-departmental committee of senior public servants, with Hamilton Southam as co-ordinator, recommended what was called the Brussels Plan. According to this plan, there would be a chairman and a board of trustees who would receive and be responsible for the funds granted by the

157

government. There would be also three additional chairmen and boards of directors, who would be responsible for the orchestra, the theatres (French and English), including programming, and the International Festival of the Arts. Because the Board of Trustees would have no responsibility for the artistic requirements of the centre, it followed, in my opinion, that it could not be expected to accept responsibility for the finances. It also seemed obvious that the Board would receive pressures from the other chairmen and their boards for financing the three organizations, but the Trustees would have no authority to correct unacceptable situations, should they occur. In addition, such an organization would be expensive and would involve duplication of responsibility. I informed Judy LaMarsh that I could not accept this plan, and that if the government persisted in pursuing it, I felt that, with the greatest of respect, a new chairman should be sought. She agreed with my view, and we went ahead with the job of organization.

The government was thoughtful and used discretion in selecting an excellent Board of Trustees including: Claude Robillard (Vice-Chairman), His Worship Donald B. Reid, Mayor of Ottawa, Son Honneur Marcel D'Amour, Mayor of Hull, Jean Boucher, Alphonse Ouimet, Grant McLean, Leonard Kitz, Mrs. Andrée Paradis, William Teron, Dr. Robertson Davies, Madeleine Gobeil, Anson McKim, Dr. Arnold Walter, and Dr. Dorothy Maud Somerset. They reflected a broad national representation, and possessed knowledge in the arts, and responsibility in business. It was important that the Mayors of Ottawa and Hull be *ex-officio* members of the Board. Other *ex-officio* members were the President of the CBC, Alphonse Ouimet, the Executive Director of the Canada Council, the late Jean Boucher, and the Chairman of the National Film Board, Grant McLean. This encouraged an affinity, understanding, and co-operation in these complementary cultural pursuits. Providing for this kind of representation in the National Arts Centre Act was, I believe, an important factor in making the centre a success.

One of the first decisions I faced was the appointment of the Director General. There were many suggestions from well-meaning people, both in and out of government. With the greatest of respect to people in the arts, not many artists possess great administrative or financial ability. Frequently, the more artistic, the less responsible one might be in these essential areas. There had never been an arts centre in Canada, and at that time there was only Lincoln Centre in New York and the centre in Los Angeles. We were next at that point, and now there is only one more, the Kennedy Centre in Washington. There was not much of an experienced talent pool from which to select a Director General, who must be able to understand the vast range of fields in the performing arts and be able to exercise administrative and financial control. His responsibilities would far exceed those of a director of a theatre, a ballet company, an orchestra, or even of an opera house–because the centre would house them all.

I went to New York to discuss the matter with my friend Tony Guthrie who agreed that there was not a person in the arts who could assume these varied responsibilities. He felt that it would be better for the centre if we appointed a person of taste and administrative ability from outside the arts field. I felt that, if we appointed someone outside the arts, the appointee should be someone from Ottawa. I believed it necessary that he or she be imbued with a love and pride for the city as the nation's capital. Because Hamilton Southam had formed the National Capital Arts Alliance, was dedicated to the principle, had brought in the consultants, and presented a plan for the centre to the government, he was an excellent candidate for the position. I was informed by External Affairs that he had been a good administrator and, if he accepted the position, External would regret his leaving.

When I first spoke to him, Hamilton was concerned, and quite properly so, because in the organizational plan I envisaged, the Director General would be the executive head and have the responsibility to the Board for the artistic, administrative, and financial requirements of the centre. I believed he would be a good appointment, and he was.

When Hamilton told me he would accept the position, I called a small ad hoc committee meeting at the Chateau Laurier, which included Robertson Davies and Dr. Arnold Walter. We decided to recommend to the Board the appointment of Hamilton Southam as Director General. This recommendation was unanimously accepted by the Board and approved by the government.

We had good fortune in filling the number-two slot–the Deputy Director General–with Mr. Bruce Corder, whose knowledge of the fine opera house at Covent Garden, where he had been trained, gave him the multi-faceted skills necessary for his position in Ottawa.

Now we had the other slots to fill. Hamilton would agree that some of the people who filled them were very good and, regrettably, some were not. Through what was a difficult period he displayed, in his choices of personnel, great patience. Eventually, a sound organization was developed.

It was obvious from the beginning that we required an orchestra, although the Montreal and Toronto Symphonies were opposed to it. When we met with senior members of their boards on several occasions, their position was that a third symphony orchestra was unnecessary because their two good ones already existed and they could play in Ottawa when required. They claimed this arrangement would have made their difficult financial situations somewhat easier. Furthermore, they resented the fact that an orchestra in Ottawa would be fully subsidized by government. Although they received subsidies through their respective provincial governments and the Canada Council, a lot of private money was needed to cover their substantial deficits. We countered this argument with the suggestion that the National Arts Centre was like any other governmental institution, such as a museum or art gallery. Thus, the National Gallery in Ottawa was similar to the National Gallery in London or Washington or the Louvre in Paris. We believed there was no difference in principle in a national centre for the performing arts. It was just a new fact, and there was a need for people to understand it. Frankly, Hamilton and I got nowhere in these meetings. I was later informed that certain members of the Toronto and Montreal Symphonies' boards requested their respective Cabinet ministers to use their influence to prevent the formation of an orchestra in the National Arts Centre. During all of this, there were further discussions on whether the orchestra should be a full-sized symphony or a smaller orchestra. Hamilton and some of his colleagues and advisers on the Canada Council favoured the smaller orchestra. I believed that, if we could afford it, we should have a large sym-

160

phony. I made an appointment for Hamilton and I to discuss the matter with Leonard Bernstein in New York. He told us that if we could afford it the larger symphony would be better because from it we could utilize smaller parts for small symphonic works; if we had a smaller symphony, we could not play the larger works. However, when we considered the political ramifications, it was obvious that it would be more appropriate to suggest a small symphony because Montreal and Toronto already had large ones. Our immediate problem was that we did not have an orchestra, whatever size, to put in the centre.

Hamilton had an inspiration – that we invite Jean-Marie Beaudet, the Vice-President of Music for the CBC, to form the orchestra. The matter was discussed with him and I made an appointment with the President of the CBC, then our colleague on the board, Alphonse Ouimet. At our meeting, Mr. Ouimet agreed that if Jean-Marie would join us, he was willing to make the appointment possible. Jean-Marie was thus seconded to the Arts Centre to be Director of Music. Our new director was as inspired as Hamilton had been when he suggested him. No one person is more responsible for the orchestra than Jean-Marie Beaudet. His ambition was to found a small symphony orchestra that would rank with the best in the world, and he held auditions throughout Canada, the United States, and Europe for that purpose. He interviewed conductors and brought to us a list of possibilities, one of whom was Mario Bernardi. The most knowledgeable member of the board on music, the late Dr. Arnold Walter, spoke of Mario for at least half an hour and recommended his appointment as conductor. When we announced Mario's appointment, many young Canadian musicians in Europe wished to return to Canada to play under his direction.

Mario's vigour, youth, musical talent, and his ability to work hard, made the orchestra a splendid one from the very beginning. I felt, and my Board agreed, that the public should not have to wait for the many years that it usually takes to develop a fine orchestra. We believed it essential that from the first concert, a fine orchestra should play. Mario made this possible. When he came to Canada as conductor and musical director of the orchestra, Mario left the post of conductor and musical director of the

Sadler's Wells Opera. He had studied in Italy, where his parents had sent him from Kirkland Lake, Ontario, when he showed musical talent at an early age, to finally gain distinction in his musical studies from the Conservatory of Venice. To Mario is due much praise for the orchestra's successes at Lincoln Centre, in Moscow, at the Bath Festival, in Versailles, at the Kennedy Centre, and in many cities and towns in Canada, and the United States.

The question of the French and English theatres for the centre was a matter of serious concern. When we knew that the Arts Centre was to be built in Ottawa, I suggested that the Stratford Company move to Ottawa after its Stratford season concluded each year. Michael Langham discussed his belief that great companies should live together, work together, and act together, and that long contracts would bring to people of the theatre a security they could not feel by doing only a summer festival. But the idea of taking the complete company to Ottawa did not meet the approval of my colleagues at Stratford. Despite the fact that the new theatre was being built in Ottawa, Michael believed that Montreal should be the choice for the development of a winter season for the Stratford company. One of the reasons for the lack of enthusiasm was that Stratford felt possessive of its fine company, which was understandable considering what the city and its people had contributed to developing the theatre. But I felt that the refusal to co-operate reflected a degree of provincialism that had been evident in discussions of what I chose to call the "development of a national theatre for Canada."

I suggested that Shakespeare be played in Stratford, and at the conclusion of the season at the end of September, the whole company be moved to Ottawa for a fall season, beginning in November, and continue through early April. The company would then move back to Stratford in late April or early May. I envisioned that the theatre in Ottawa would do classical plays other than Shakespeare, and also contemporary plays of great merit. Players would have long contracts, with time allowed for them to play in New York City and London, in order to offer the change and stimulation that every good actor requires. From a standing start, and with no agreement on the Board, there began a movement on the Stratford Board, led by my friend Floyd

162

Chalmers, that the idea might be an effective theatrical pursuit, and in Canada's interest as well. I should point out that when I first raised this idea at Stratford, I had no inkling that I might be associated with the National Arts Centre. Certainly, I had no idea that I would be its founding Chairman.

After many months of informal discussion, we finally agreed that, should we be able to organize a financial solution, the matter would be brought back to the Board for formal consideration. The crunch came at a meeting in Toronto. Stratford's Jean Gascon, Bill Wyley, the late General Manager of Stratford, and Hamilton Southam and I for the centre, talked until the early hours of the morning. It was obvious that, certainly for the first year, the centre could not afford the substantial amount required – a very rough estimate was $750,000. As an alternative, we proposed bringing to our respective boards a proposal wherein two of the plays opening the festival, and two of the plays from the former season, be brought to Ottawa, so that there would be four plays from Stratford included in the program at the Arts Centre. Some of us believed that the arrangement was the beginning of what would eventually lead to the Stratford theatre moving to Ottawa. And thus the name Stratford National Theatre was used. As Chairman of the NAC and with my Board's concurrence, the Stratford Board was invited to Ottawa to meet with us, and a contract was signed. Because I had accepted, by then, the chairmanship of the National Arts Centre, I resigned my position on the Stratford Board.

The plays from Stratford that have come to Ottawa have been most successful. But I think it regrettable that more steps for a national theatre have not been taken and that the idea, which some of us believed might place Canada in a position of theatrical world eminence, has not been developed.

In these early years of the Arts Centre, our "hits," in my opinion, included the orchestra, our "runs" were in the programming department, and our "errors" were in the French and English theatre productions, as good as some of them were. To achieve its national purpose, I believed, and still do, that a French theatre of international importance is essential for the centre. A great step forward in French and English theatre has just been made in the recent appointment of Jean Gascon as

Director of Theatre for the centre. It is hoped that with his appointment these ambitions will be realized.

The highlight, the grand culmination of our months and years of effort was, of course, the official opening of the National Arts Centre in June of 1969.

Planning for the opening began early. The Board and staff had decided that the building should be opened on a Saturday, when the public would be invited to attend the opening ceremonies. The formal opening on Monday night could then be an artistic presentation, uncluttered by speeches and tributes.

If we thought we had problems before, organizing opening night set a new high. As a Crown Corporation, we were responsible for issuing invitations to government officials, performing arts representatives throughout Canada, and distinguished people in the arts generally. Also, we felt it essential to keep at least one-third of the tickets for sale to the public. With only 2,200 seats in the Opera House, we kept over 700 for the public, to be sold at the box office. There were then only 1,400 invitations or only 700 couples. Our first-draft list of invitations contained thousands of names. Only the patience of my Opening Night Committee, the diligence of Hamilton Southam, and the sympathetic knowledge of Carl Lochnan, then head of protocol in the Secretary of State's department, kept us sane and resolved the problems. We decided that throughout the Opening Festival, from June 2 to June 14, everyone would pay for his seat, regardless of position.

At the Saturday afternoon ceremonies, it was estimated that around 50,000 people came to see the building. The speeches were short and the speakers few. After the Minister of Public Works, Mr. Arthur Laing, and the Secretary of State, Mr. Gerard Pelletier, who spoke briefly, Prime Minister Trudeau turned the deed of the building over to me as Chairman, and I made a few remarks. It was a happy and festive celebration for the throngs of people. There were only two small, unfortunate mishaps. During my remarks, the microphone broke down. Fortunately I was amused, and said simply: "I hope the sound and electronics work better on the stages of the building than at this particular moment in the foyer." Later, when I took the Prime Minister through the building, unhappily I chose a wrong door and proceeded to lead him down a stairway. I quickly recognized my mistake and turned around to ascend. But we were so crowded with photographers and newspaper people that it was almost impossible. Eventually, we got the Prime Minister's tour of the building back on the rails. My friends of the press, however, were gallant in their later reports, saying that "a high official of the NAC made the blunder." They did not name me. It was a gentle and appreciated gesture.

I had occasion, recently, to reminisce with David Haber, who was our Director of Programming, about the opening. Referring to the Saturday festivities, he said: "Music filled the foyers, choirs sang on the staircase, rehearsals were interrupted by tours, bands played on various outdoor terraces, balloons were set off, and after approximately twelve exhausting hours, this fantastic day came to an end with a magnificent display of fireworks. For some, this was the most eventful day in the history of the performing arts in Canada."

David also recalled his recommendation to the Director General and his other colleagues, which was subsequently approved by the Board: "An original, exciting, possibly controversial attraction should open the centre, an attraction that would shatter the eye, the ear, and even the mind of the public. An opera is not possible, but a magnificent new ballet could be produced." David was the catalyst in commissioning a new work. He began discussions with Celia Franca and her colleagues in the National Ballet of Canada with the objective of achieving a new dimension in choreography for the 1970s with original music and contemporary designs. It was his hope that this would be a "creation that would turn all heads toward Ottawa and the opening of the National Arts Centre." And so Roland Petit of Paris was engaged to do the choreography, Iannis Xenakis, the Greek composer, was commissioned to write a score for orchestra and electronic tape, and Victor Vasarely and his son Yvaral were asked to create the visual effects. David expressed the intention: "Not only will dancers move in front of scenery, but the scenery will move along with the dancers. All in all, we should work toward the contemporary interpretation of the word ballet – the perfect marriage of movement, music, and design."

The result was *Kraanerg*, indeed a controversial ballet and one of the century's most contemporary. The style and staging used has been copied by just about every choreographer in the world since 1969. David believes that "The mounting of *Kraanerg* showed the world what the magnificent new Opera House could do, the effects that could be created on the best stage in Canada, and one of the best stages in the world, the acoustics and endless capabilities of the front-of-house, the distinct comfort and facilities for the performers backstage." There was a parallel score recorded electronically and played on speakers around the house with the symphony. There were some harsh reviews, but Clive Barnes of the *New York Times* wrote that the score was one of the finest scores for ballet of the twentieth century. When I saw Barnes some years later in Palm Beach, I told him how pleased we were with this critique because of the controversy on the dissonance of sound and the extremely modern choreography of *Kraanerg*. I thanked him for enabling us to counter other criticism with his statement.

French theatre was to open the festival's second night. Le Théâtre du Nouveau Monde was asked to produce something and they chose *Lysistrata*, based on the Greek comedy, but told in French contemporary musical form. It was a tremendous success and showed how the theatre could adapt to complicated theatrical treatments, lighting effects, and how splendid the acoustics were for the spoken word. It was a pleasurable and theatrically provocative experience for both the audience and the players. It was a night of triumph for Michel Tremblay, the Director André Brassard, who wrote the score, and the stunning Denise Filiatrault, whose performance was most unusual and exciting. Now the Opera House and the Theatre were open.

The third evening marked the opening of the Studio, the avant-garde, experimental theatre of the complex. Jack Winter, a young Toronto playwright, presented a controversial play called *Party Game*. It may not have been the artistic success that we had wished, but it did show the multi-faceted theatrical uses and the incredible experimental potential of this studio theatre. As David Haber described it: "*Party Game* was performed everywhere and the audience sat everywhere. The action took place on the normal floor, in the balcony, down a twelve-foot pit—and some of the audience found itself going down into the pit with the performers. The audience sat in islands, in clusters, all around and above. The production showed that the Studio had no limitation and, inventively used, could be a most exciting area.''

The next opening was of the exquisitely intimate Salon. It opened on the Festival's fourth night, and some of Canada's finest chamber music ensembles were invited: the Manitoba Consort of Winnipeg, the Orford Quartet of Toronto, the Duo Pach of Fredericton, and the Casenti Players of Vancouver.

The Opening Festival was planned to provide quality in the performing arts in Canada, and also to demonstrate not only the beauty of the centre, but its splendid technical facilities as well.

Kraanerg was followed during the opening festivities with the National Ballet of Canada's presentations of *Romeo and Juliet* and *Swan Lake*. The Montreal Symphony played, with guests Jon Vickers and Regine Crespin. Seiji Ozawa conducted the Toronto Symphony. In all of this there was the all-important consideration of young people as well. Monique Leyrac, Gordon Lightfoot, and Pop Electronique helped make clear that young people could come to the Arts Centre comfortably and casually. In beautiful surroundings they could hear the best in soft and hard rock music, fine folk, and other popular music forms.

The Vancouver Playhouse brought George Ryga's *The Ecstasy of Rita Joe* to the Theatre. At this play, a stunning satire and critique of the social abuses Canadian Indians suffer, Mr. Jean Chrétien, then the distinguished and youthful Minister of Indian and Northern Affairs, was in the audience. The fact that the minister responsible for Indian affairs was present gave emphasis to the importance of the play, which is a cry against the injustice inflicted on native people by a seemingly uncaring society. He appeared to enjoy the play.

Party Game was followed in the Studio by the gifted Gabriel Charpentier's mini-opera, *Orphée*.

These days were full of enthusiasm, excitement, and satisfaction – and exhaustion. The staff was superb. Audrey and I had a wonderful time, although a somewhat tiring one. We entertained on many nights during these hectic weeks. Every now and then we found ourselves in unusual dilemmas which, if not serious, were momentarily complicating. On the first night, we had arranged for Their Excellencies, the Governor General Roland Michener and Mrs. Michener to receive my Board, senior staff, and all those who had been responsible for the development of the centre. We expected that Their Excellencies would be the host and hostess of the evening, but just after the intermission, His Excellency made it patently clear that he expected Audrey and me to be the hostess and host. Accordingly, in the Salon, at intermission, I presented the ladies and gentlemen to Their Excellencies and everything proceeded satisfactorily. The problem emerged at the conclusion of the performance when Audrey and I were faced, as the newly-appointed hostess and host, with an immediate problem of protocol in seating approximately 150 distinguished guests, including Their Excellencies, the Prime Minister, various ministers of the Crown, and all the other VIPs whose presence graced this significant moment. It had to be done quickly and Audrey and I, after a momentary huddle, appropriated the two centre tables and invited His Excellency to sit on Audrey's right and Her Excellency on my right at the adjoining table. We then sat the Prime Minister and the Vice-Chairman of the centre with Paul Hébert, and his wife, at an appropriate table, and Gerard Pelletier, the Secretary of State, and his wife, with a senior Board member at another appropriate table. From then on we let the social chips fall where they might. We hoped it proved satisfactory from the point of view of protocol. Whether it did or not was probably not too important, as it turned out, fortunately, to be a happy conclusion to a superb evening.

On the second night, at the opening of the Theatre, we had arranged for place cards for Their Excellencies, the Prime Minister, and other distinguished guests. Inasmuch as we had received some criticism because the supper party the evening before had been given in the Salon, implying an exclusivity from the throngs outside in the foyer, we decided that Their Excellencies, the Prime Minister, and our other notable guests would be seated above the stairs in the foyer in front of the Bonnet doors. This evening, we invited all of the members of the diplomatic corps, and their wives, and many other distinguished guests, to attend the party in the foyer outside the Salon. Audrey and I were determined we would not have the same problem this evening and, accordingly, arranged for place cards.

We reserved the correct place for the Prime Minister, but we were surprised when he did not arrive for supper. We sent scouts out all over the building to look for him, but he was not to be found. I was later informed that he had been in the stage area, discussing ballet with some of the dancers of the company. After a considerable time, General Trudeau (no relation to the Prime Minister) sat in the place of the Prime Minister. Imagine my dismay when, what seemed to be ages later, the Prime Minister finally appeared, walking through the crowds toward our table, where there was now no place for him. General Trudeau made a gallant gesture, took his plate and dashed off through the multitudes. Unable to find a waiter, I literally ran to the buffet table for knives, forks, plates, butter, etc. and, in seconds before his arrival, had them properly placed. The Prime Minister's place looked unsullied and expectant when he arrived.

These moments of confusion over protocol were not in the same category as the situation that occurred when *Party Game* was presented. Our policy that the board of governors should not interfere with the programming was to cause me several moments of embarrassment. When the play opened in the Studio on the third night, I suspected there could be painful and embarrassing moments in this drama dealing with the Nazi regime in Germany. I made discreet inquiries about the content. Assured that nothing in the play could be considered upsetting to the Government of West Germany, I reassured the German Ambassador at a cocktail party before the opening, when he questioned me about it.

As the play unfolded, I realized that there might be a problem. The pungent, virulent anti-Nazi dialogue and film seemed to indict the whole German people with painful scenes that stirred my own memories of the thirties and forties.

Early the next morning I telephoned the German Ambassador who graciously received me after breakfast. I apologized for having misinformed him. My host was formally grateful for my call and assured me that he had not been upset by the performance. He did not think the play was an indictment of the German people because of the anti-Nazi posture of his government and his people. It is regrettable that I can never forget or forgive the horrendous atrocities.

By November, five months after it opened, I think it is fair to say that the centre had achieved its main purpose. It was a spectacular showcase for the finest of the performing arts of the nation. It had a splendid orchestra, which was already perhaps the most prestigious in Canada, a box office percentage high enough to be almost unknown in a complex of this size and kind, and was playing its three houses almost every night of the week. There had been many problems along the way. Fortunately, there were none that turned out to be insoluble.

By late fall of 1969, I believed that I had completed the job the government had requested of me: to organize and set up the administration for the development of the National Arts Centre. After the years of planning, six months of a tremendously successful operation, and with splendid programming planned for the next six months, I felt the centre "really could not miss." I decided to discuss the matter with the minister, Mr. Pelletier. I felt that a new Chairman should take a new look at the centre. It was one thing to undertake the organization of an enterprise of this magnitude from its administrative beginning, and quite another to oversee its administration on a continuing basis. Also, my doctors had advised me that I should "take to the sun" for six months, and I was still involved in my many other business and organizational pursuits. I asked the minister to permit me to retire when it was convenient to him, assuring him that there was no urgency on my part. He was most gracious and understanding, and on my retirement, generous in referring to my contribution to the Arts Centre in his public statements and to me personally. The members of my Board indicated their regrets at my leaving. In their letters, and in other expressions, they gave evidence of what they felt had been a sincere and worthy effort on my part in the establishment of the National Arts Centre. There was also great warmth and friendship expressed by many members of the staff. They were perhaps overly kind, because all of these people, through their splendid efforts, had played an enormous role in making the National Arts Centre of today a focal point in the cultural life of the national capital and of the nation.

Chapter VIII

The House of Israel

My personal Zionist belief is quite natural for me, acquired, as if by osmosis, in my mother's and father's house.

I am a Zionist. I accept the aims of the Jerusalem Program:*

The unity of the Jewish people and the centrality of Israel in Jewish life;

The ingathering of the Jewish people in its historic homeland Eretz Israel through Aliyah from all countries;

The strengthening of the State of Israel which is based on the prophetic vision of justice and peace;

The preservation of the identity of the Jewish people through the fostering of Jewish and Hebrew education and of Jewish spiritual and cultural values;

The protection of Jewish rights everywhere.

This statement, by itself, however, is an over-simplification. There are other important concepts that require consideration.

I agree with the belief expressed by my dear friend, the late

*The Jerusalem Program was approved by the 27th World Zionist Congress, June 19, 1968.

171

Moshe Sharett, which considers that loyalty to one's country must include other loyalties: loyalty to one's family, to the traditions and culture of one's people and loyalty to one's faith. It follows quite naturally that with this understanding, there was never a problem regarding loyalty to my country, Canada, irrespective of my ties with Israel. Surely, regardless of one's particular faith, there is a requirement for these other loyalties in order to be a good Canadian. This is basic to the philosophy that Prime Minister Trudeau expressed on Parliament Hill on Canada Day, July 1, 1976, when he said:

> ...It is not only a gift to you new Canadians of your share in this country, a gift of every right and privilege which belongs to Canadians, but it's also an enjoinder and a prayer that you share also the obligations of Canadians. And these obligations are part of our traditions. They are our desire to respect and tolerate all the differences which can exist between us. Not only tolerate but encourage them because we know that Canada's wealth, Canada's richness, Canadians' fulfillment as a people, lies in our diversity and not in our homogeneity. And that is why Canadians encourage every other Canadian to maintain their traditions, to keep their language in what we call a policy of multi-culturalism, to bring the wealth of your personality to Canada, but not to forget the beautiful things that you or your ancestors might have received in other parts of the world....

There must also be an understanding of the two basic philosophies of Zionism, as enunciated in the great debate between Nahum Goldmann and the late David Ben-Gurion. Dr. Goldmann believes that there must be an undertaking in Zionism to ensure the survival of the Jewish people, wherever they may be. He affirms the centrality of Israel in the Jewish world as "The brightest star in the Jewish firmament." He affirms also that one is a Zionist if he participates in these objectives, wherever he resides. Mr. Ben-Gurion, on the contrary, enunciated the belief that one could not be a Zionist unless he could live with full civil and religious liberties and this could only be achieved in the land of his forefathers – Israel.

These, then, are the Zionist options. The fact that I happen to believe in Dr. Goldmann's philosophy does not preclude or negate the position of Mr. Ben-Gurion. The main point is to know and to do what one's conscience dictates.

As the need for funds for Israel became greater, to some extent there was a progressive loss of understanding of the important truths of Zionism, its nobility and never-changing purpose, from Herzl's time – and before. This is not meant for a moment to suggest that it is not vital to raise funds for Israel's survival, but it is meant to suggest that the sale of Israel bonds, the United Jewish Appeal, or other important agencies which assist the state financially are, in fact, the instruments which implement the cause of Zionism.

Looking back, it was singularly fortunate that my father's and mother's house contained the joys and disappointments, the exhilaration and the frustration of their work for a Jewish state. It was a rare privilege granted to so few to meet some of the significant personalities of the century who, before the State of Israel became a reality on November 29, 1947, had done so much to help create it. My parents' house opened a doorway to yet another house – the eternal home of our people, Israel. In their house I met many of the great people of Israel, the people of my father's generation, who began much of the work carried on, years later, by the people of my own generation. From the day of the proclamation of independence, Jews outside of Israel would meet a new test and challenge, possibly the greatest in the long history of our people. It is inevitable that the State will survive – and just as inevitable that the strength needed to sustain it is and will be greater than history could have conceived.

In 1948, after Canada had delayed recognition of the new State of Israel for many months, I went with some of my colleagues to see Prime Minister Louis St. Laurent. Not only the Jewish community, but many non-Jewish, liberal-minded people throughout Canada were concerned that Canada's failure to recognize the State was prejudicial to its future. Some of us also felt that it was prejudicial to Canada's international prestige, especially in view of the fact that Canada had played such an important role in the creation of the State, primarily through the efforts and imagination of Lester Pearson at the United Nations, when he was Under-Secretary of State for External Affairs. These points were made clear to Mr. St. Laurent who was, as usual, courteous and dignified. But we did not receive a satisfactory reply. I argued that as a sovereign nation Canada had to do what it thought was right, regardless of the attitudes of the United Kingdom. I took a strong position. One of Mr. St. Laurent's assistants informed me that the Prime Minister was pleased by my forthrightness and direct approach at the meeting, yet another indication of the great stature of the man I held in such high regard.

Moshe Sharett, then Foreign Minister of the State, arrived in Ottawa to meet with the Prime Minister and senior members of the Cabinet and to press the case for recognition. I accompanied Mr. Sharett on his difficult mission, and was deeply impressed by his presentation, which was brilliant, incisive, and intellectually magnificent. While it lacked emotion, it created a fullness of understanding, from both a political and a humanistic point of view that had not existed before.

Then, finally it happened—Canada fully and formally recognized the State of Israel in August 1949. In November of that same year, Avraham Harman arrived in Montreal as Consul General, the first of a distinguished line of representatives to Canada.

No one could symbolize the State of Israel in his own being more effectively than "Abe" Harman. His vitality, force, and will to overcome all odds were always evident. His sheer determination "touched" all who met him. Abe later served as Ambassador to the United States from 1959 to 1968 and is now the distinguished President of the Hebrew University in Jerusalem. There, he and his colleagues have developed a splendid university, in academic terms, and have regenerated a Hebrew culture to bring to the world again in our time what our forefathers brought to the world centuries ago. As the new buildings rise, as remarkable in number as they are in design, so rises his indomitable spirit for further accomplishment.

All those years back he came to Ottawa as one of his first "ports of call." I met him and took him to a small hall where he delivered a fiery call to Jews, and his words sounded to the very

174

depths of our spirits. Abe Harman set a pattern in the Canadian Jewish community that continues to this day. It was a pattern based on dedication and moral force that engaged the hearts and minds of all those fortunate enough to meet him.

Finally, it was agreed that Canada and Israel would exchange representatives at the ambassadorial level. Eliyahu Elat, who was Ambassador to the United States, came to Ottawa to meet influential Canadian government officials to work out the details. Audrey and I had had the pleasure of meeting Eliyahu and his wife in Washington, where we held a reception for them to which we invited a number of Canada's senior officials.

Then, an embassy was acquired in Ottawa and made ready for the arrival of Michael Comay and his wife Joan. They arrived in the summer of 1953 with their two children Jill and Jochanan, accompanied on the train by Samuel Bronfman, then President of the Canadian Jewish Congress, and Eddie Gelber, President of the Zionist Organization of Canada. Audrey and I met them at the station with hundreds of Ottawa people who wished, with us, to mark the day as a historic one.

Michael's qualifications were seemingly endless: great intellectual strength, combined with total dedication and determination. With respect to their selflessness, Michael and Joan were a microcosm of the people of Israel. Michael had been a lawyer in Capetown, South Africa, and Joan an architect. When the war came, he enlisted as a private in the South African army, and eventually found himself in Montgomery's army in North Africa. His family, and then Michael, had been ardent Zionists, so during his North African wartime years he went to Palestine each time his leave permitted. Michael rose steadily through the ranks and was discharged at war's end as a Major. He went to Palestine and simply cabled Joan to meet him there. There could not have been a better choice than Michael and Joan as their country's representatives. They were popular in the diplomatic corps and created among the Jewish and non-Jewish communities in Canada a prestige for the new embassy. Michael, through these sometimes difficult days, chose an eclectic style that was highly successful. Without ever prejudicing a principle, he chose the best method and source to accomplish the objectives he set. There was no meeting of Jews or non-Jews that was too small for him to attend. He would drive forty or fifty miles to a church hall to speak to fifteen or twenty people and tell them about the emerging state. Joan, too, would take speaking commitments wherever in North America they might be.

Some of the situations that developed in those days were most interesting, if somewhat ironic. When some of the "glamour" of the incoming ambassador began to wear off, Michael and I found, to our astonishment, that certain important Canadian Jewish people and organizations believed they had been somewhat slighted because now the ambassador represented and spoke for the state on occasions when, formerly, they would have done so. Michael was a fine diplomat and these matters were not only overcome, but uncertainty was transformed into deep confidence.

Michael was one of the people who influenced my life, too. He enthusiastically supported the suggestion that I become the President of the Zionist Organization of Canada, and would lecture me at length on this subject. One night, as we sat outside the Chateau Laurier in my car until about 3:00 in the morning, he finally convinced me. I became the President of the Zionist Organization of Canada in 1958. As I saw it, the presidency had three main requirements. First, it was necessary for the organization to co-operate completely with other significant national Jewish organizations, primarily the Canadian Jewish Congress, and with the Embassy of Israel, if it was to speak with knowledge and responsibility. Second, it was of vital importance to have a better-informed Jewish community so that the full effect of the Zionist philosophy would be more meaningful, not only for the present generation, but also for the next. It was therefore necessary to do everything that we could to foster these attitudes in the universities and among young Jewish people throughout the country. This would have the further effect of increasing the financial assistance that Israel required, because understanding fosters assistance. Third, there was a requirement to organize the other national Zionist organizations into one unified and coordinated entity so that the full thrust of Zionist effort would be more effective. In all of these matters, Michael and the embassy were most helpful and, through the auspices of the Zionist Organization of Canada, we tried to make "the road" easier for him and his associates. We were able to do this because of our knowledge of the organizations and the people, Jewish and non-Jewish, in the national capital, and throughout the country.

From the beginning of my presidency, "my road" was made easier by the co-operation of Samuel Bronfman, not only in his role as President of the Canadian Jewish Congress, but also by our long friendship. He made it clear to everyone how pleased he was when I was elected President and that there would now be a close relationship between the Canadian Zionist Organization and the Canadian Jewish Congress. This arrangement was consolidated through the generous efforts of Saul Hayes, the authoritative Director of the Canadian Jewish Congress. Saul and I had been at university together. He could bring to important situations his intellectual gifts and his vast knowledge of the Jewish community in Canada. Saul always did his "homework" exceedingly well and, maybe even more important, he possessed strong Jewish attitudes. Although many people felt that Saul Hayes was the voice of Samuel Bronfman (because of Sam's great influence), I think it is fairer to speak of the close co-operation that existed between Sam and Saul. They were a splendid team, and of tremendous assistance to me and my colleagues in the Zionist family. More important, however, was the fact that together we managed to speak with a unified voice on behalf of the Canadian Jewish community.

Working toward a better-informed Jewish community, I tried, during my presidency, to speak to Jewish communities throughout the country. The usual procedure was that some kind person in a given community would hold a reception on Saturday night, no matter how late I arrived. There was usually a Sunday luncheon and then a dinner, with my speech Sunday night. I would then take as early a plane as possible on Monday morning in the hope of being back in my office by 10:00 A.M. I met so many like-minded, encouraging people, that I never considered those trips to be work, as such.

One of the most successful trips occurred when Dr. Nahum Goldmann, President of the World Zionist Organization, Samuel Bronfman, President of the Canadian Jewish Congress, and I travelled from Winnipeg to Vancouver to raise funds for the United Jewish Appeal. To be on the same speaking program as

Nahum Goldmann is, to say the least, a self-deflating process. Knowing one's limitations in speech-making, and knowing that one is to speak night after night with one of the great orators of the world, does not make for an "inflated ego"–but it does create humility! To have spent time with Goldmann over a quiet weekend, as we did in Banff, was memorable. Goldmann is a handsome man, his shock of grey hair heightening the sparkle and deep intelligence of his grey eyes. His incisive mind, his tremendous knowledge of politics, philosophy, and literature, and his great skill as raconteur make him an unforgettable man.

A memorable vignette of Goldmann stemmed from a call we received while in Banff. It was suggested that Sam, Goldmann, and I visit a reception for a very affluent gentleman who was celebrating his wedding anniversary. It was suggested that our attendance might induce the gentleman to make a much larger contribution than had been his custom over the years. I knew when I received the message what Goldmann's reaction would be. Refusing the invitation, he smiled and said, "Lawrence, it has not been easy to bring the State to the point it is at, but somehow or other we shall be able to manage to build it without the assistance of one who did not know we existed up to this point...we shall build it without him."

There were also many important conferences to attend in various parts of the world. One of the most significant was the Jerusalem Conference of October 1953, called by Prime Minister David Ben-Gurion. There was a large international attendance, and one of the main issues to be decided was whether or not the Israel Bond program, which Ben-Gurion had organized with American Jewish leaders in 1951, should be expanded to a world-wide effort. It had been a contentious issue since the Jerusalem Economic Conference of September 1950, when Ben-Gurion persuaded American Jewish leaders of the need for a bond issue to raise investment funds for Israel's economic development. That conference had adopted a four-point program of financing: continued raising, in larger amounts, of "philanthropic" funds through the United Jewish Appeal; the new bond drive in America; direct private-sector investments in Israel's economy; and inter-governmental or international grants and loans. This conference, three years later, was to decide on Ben-Gurion's recommendation that the bond drive become international. Opponents of the idea feared that a large, aggressive bond-sales organization might prejudice gift dollars for the United Israel Appeal.

The purposes of each organization were obvious, as was the need for both. The United Israel Appeal finances the absorption and integration of immigrants into Israel, a most costly affair. The Israel bond concept was and is to raise funds for the industrial development of Israel. These interest-bearing bonds would provide funds that would be borrowed from World Jewry.

It seemed obvious to me that, even though there might be some risk involved, as far as the United Jewish Appeal was concerned, both fund organizations were vital to Israel. I agreed with Canada's acceptance of the Israel Bond Organization. In all, thirty-three countries, including Canada, voted to accept the proposal. Since its beginning in 1951, the Israel Bond Organization has raised tremendous amounts. Subsequent events have proved that the organization has been vital to Israel's development and has not prejudiced the United Jewish Appeal, which has gone from strength to strength.

Another highlight was the first Canadian Mission to Israel. One evening, I read in *The Jerusalem Post* of an important mission to Israel from the United States. Reading the article, I was surprised to realize that there had not yet been such a mission from Canada. Early the next morning, I telephoned Sam Bronfman, suggesting that we lead a mission together, under the auspices of the Zionist Organization of Canada and the Canadian Jewish Congress. I suggested that we invite outstanding representatives of the Canadian Jewish community to join us. Sam immediately replied, "Lawrence, I think this is a splendid idea. When shall we go?" I said that because of business, it would be more convenient for me to leave after the Christmas season and, possibly, this might be a better time for many members of the group. He agreed, and we set the date for the latter part of December 1959, and early January 1960. This short conversation was an accurate reflection of Sam's ability to make quick and responsible decisions. He did not refer to his calendar, which must have included many important meetings. When he felt there was a priority, the decision was taken, although these were very busy days for him.

Immediately, the wheels were put into motion through both

of our organizations, and in a very short time we had acceptances from a distinguished and geographically representative group across the country. Most of the arrangements in Israel were made through Teddy Kollek, who was then in charge of Prime Minister Ben-Gurion's office. He spent a tremendous amount of time to ensure the success of the mission, knowing that if it were successful, it would pave the way for many more. Even in the arrangements he made for us, we were aware of the qualities that have made this man one of the legendary figures of Israel. Teddy Kollek is a large man, in mind and in spirit. He exudes energy, vibrance, and great humour. His full laugh and forthright manner evoke confidence. He is loquacious and yet extremely discerning. His range of interests has been wide and varied, from international undertakings, emanating from the Prime Minister's office, to the splendid museum in Jerusalem to being Mayor of Jerusalem, a task which in itself must be one of the most complicated in the world. Each venture has been marked by great success.

A plan was made through Teddy's office for the mission to meet with President Ben-Zwi. The President and his wife gave a reception for us, a happy occasion marked by two personal incidents. The President told me how he had visited with my father on a trip to Ottawa years before. He told me at first hand the story of how he had found Father's office in our store, which was at that time not very large, but finding it had required some skill on his part because of a stairway that misled him. The second incident presented something of a personal problem for me. President Zwi told his aide that it might be more informal for his guests if I, rather than the aide, presented them. Because I had met many in the mission only the day before, I was afraid I wouldn't remember their names. I remonstrated with the aide, but he stated that this was the President's wish. There was no doubt that "that was that." I asked him for the list so that I could study it for a few moments in a small sitting room adjoining the reception room. It was understood by the aide and me that the line would be formed in the order of the list. He would stand directly behind me, so that if I missed a name he could whisper it in my ear. I know that it could never happen again but, to my surprise, I got through the whole list and said reasonably correct things to the President about most of the people I introduced. Everyone had a relaxing time.

Through Teddy's good offices, we also met many of the Cabinet ministers and spent a substantial amount of time with the Prime Minister. We visited many Kibbutzim and at each one Sam and I said a few words. We were greeted everywhere with a generosity that was touching. Before we left, we met with the late Pinchas Sapir, the sturdy, formidable Minister of Finance. Mr. Sapir had the ability to "say it as it was" in his rugged, resolute, and determined way. Sometimes one was more than a little surprised by the directness of his statements, but in the years of his responsibility in this most difficult ministry these qualities were necessary. His passing was a great blow to Israel at such a critical moment in her history. Before we left Israel, the mission had informed Mr. Sapir that it would accept responsibility for setting up the Canada-Israel Development Corporation as a vehicle for Canadian investment in Israel. Over the years, it has done well and has made a significant contribution to the State. Our first mission from Canada was a successful one, and the first of many to follow.

These were times, for me too, of new-found feelings about Israel. Some small situations brought with them dramatic overtones. For example, on a rainy morning in May 1954, the telephone rang at 7:30. It was Michael Comay, asking if I could come over to the embassy right away. I was surprised, but I said "of course." I threw on a pair of old slacks, heavy rubber-soled boots, a turtleneck, and an old raincoat. When I arrived at the embassy, Michael was waiting in the teeming rain, also wearing a raincoat. He said, "Lawrence, for the first time we will raise the flag on Israel soil in Canada at our new embassy. Today is the sixth anniversary of the State." Solemnly, hand over hand, we raised Israel's flag and said the historical Jewish prayer of thanksgiving, a shecheyonu: "Blessed art Thou, O Lord our God, King of the universe, who has kept us in life, and hast preserved us, and enabled us to reach this season." When we went inside and had our scrambled eggs and coffee, I mentioned to Michael the particular significance of this moment for me. I recounted for him the parade of all the Jews of the city, led by my grandfather, Moses Bilsky, holding my hand as a small child at the time of the Balfour Declaration in 1917. We considered the sacrifice, the lives lost in the holocaust, and the miracle that had created Israel. We also felt the privilege that was given to us to raise Israel's flag on her soil at the embassy in Canada's capital.

After four years, Michael returned to Israel. Later, he was appointed permanent representative to the United Nations, where he served for over seven years, a tribute to his tremendous success in this difficult position. Michael was succeeded in Ottawa as Ambassador by Arthur Lourie, who, with his highly intelligent wife Jeanette, carried on where Michael and Joan left off. They arrived in the summer of 1957. I suppose that the most significant characteristic setting Arthur apart from most other men is the fact that he is a gentleman in the most complete sense. Then, in the summer of 1960, Yaacov Herzog and his wonderful Penina came to the embassy. Yaacov was the son of the former Chief Rabbi there. He had the distinction himself of being an ordained rabbi. In addition, he had graduated in Law from the Hebrew University. But even this was not enough for Yaacov. His thirst for even more knowledge led him, during his busy days as Ambassador in Canada, to study in the early hours so that before he returned to Israel he had received his doctorate in Laws from the University of Ottawa.

Knowing the Herzogs was a privilege. When I questioned Yaacov on a biblical reference, he would relate a commentary from the Talmud. His knowledge was so great, his explanations simple and poignant, yet so full of meaning, that I was given a whole new understanding of biblical ideas. But it made me recognize my own lack of knowledge in the vast store of ideas for those, like Yaacov, who had taken years to search for them. When Yaacov left Ottawa to return to Israel, he became Director General of Golda Meir's ministry. On one of my visits to Israel during that time, he insisted on giving a dinner party for me and was much too complimentary in his observations of my efforts. It was a serious blow to his friends, and to Israel, when he became seriously ill and died in 1972 at the age of fifty-one. Golda Meir in her autobiography *My Life* pays tribute to Yaacov by describing him as being among the most intelligent, sophisticated men she had ever met. The embassy continued its successes with the appointments of well-qualified ambassadors, including the Avners, the Eshels, the Evrons, and the Merons. They added lustre and distinction to those days as do the Shalevs today.

Interlaced with my Zionist activities in Canada were my many visits to Israel, during some of which I had the privilege of meeting with Mr. Ben-Gurion. I recall one day waiting in his outer office to see him after certain of my colleagues in Israel had made an appointment for me. This appointment had been made without informing me beforehand and when I was told, I was somewhat distressed. I did not want to take his time in his over-busy days, but they believed the Prime Minister would want to spend a few moments with the President of the Zionist Organization off Canada. It was an extremely hot day in the summer – and it can be extremely hot in Jerusalem at that time of year. I had worn a very light-weight blue blazer and kept my tie in my jacket. In the ante-room I put on my tie. When Mr. Ben-Gurion opened the door to receive me, his first observation was, "Lawrence, when you come to my office, why do you wear a tie?" I replied, "Prime Minister, I am a Canadian who has been granted an interview with the Prime Minister of Israel." Israelis, and particularly those of the Labour Party (MAPAI), do not wear ties, believing that the practice is symbolic of restrictiveness. Symbolically, therefore, not wearing a tie is a statement, in a small way, of the freedom for which all Israelis must strive.

Over steaming tea with lemon in a glass and the inevitable sweet coffee cake, the Prime Minister went on to enquire if I was taking lessons in Hebrew. He was shocked when I told him I was not, and he proceeded to tell me that he did not believe that anyone who did not speak Hebrew should be a Zionist leader, particularly in an important country. He felt that without an understanding of Hebrew, one could not begin to understand the culture of the Jewish people. There was little question in his mind that I was an assimilated Jew who could not give the kind of Hebrew cultural leadership that he felt was requisite to this kind of post. I told him that I agreed with his philosophy but, regrettably for Israel, and probably for me, I had been elected to do the job and I would do the best I could.

It was not until he visited Canada some years later during the Goldmann-Ben-Gurion debate that the Prime Minister accepted me. There had been the great international debate on the question "What is a Zionist?" As the President of the Zionist Organization of Canada, there could have been no *raison d'être* for my job if I had not agreed completely with Dr. Goldmann. When the Prime Minister came to Canada, three speakers addressed a tremendous audience at the Queen Elizabeth Hotel in Montreal: Ben-Gurion, Sam Bronfman, and me. Because of the controversy, I knew I would have to state my position. I knew also that it had to be stated with respect to the Prime Minister, in my opinion the greatest Jew of our century. It was a difficult speech, but I gave it as well as I could. After the meeting, because I had publicly taken issue with him, he was extremely pleased. He said, "Now I know that you are the son of your father." After his return to Jerusalem, he sent me his photograph with a most generous statement over his signature: "To Lawrence Freiman, leader of Canadian Zionism and bearer of a great family tradition. With best wishes. D. Ben-Gurion, Jerusalem, 4.9.61." I quote his statement pridefully. It is something to treasure for Audrey and myself, for our children and theirs.

In these years, the Zionist Organization of Canada had great success in raising funds for Israel. At this time the United Israel Appeal came under the "umbrella" of the ZOC and we were entrusted with the responsibility of setting up the United Israel Appeal organization in co-operation with leaders of other organizations, particularly the Canadian Jewish Congress. It is a matter of record that funds, including not only the United Israel Appeal, but State of Israel Bonds, and all institutions for Israel, had increased tremendously. At the Convention of 1964, held in Montreal, my family felt, and I finally agreed with them, that with the increased responsibility in my business and in my other undertakings, two terms as President of the ZOC were enough. In the light of their concern for my health, I notified my colleagues that I could not stand for the presidency for a third term. They flattered me by their insistence, but I was adamant in my refusal – until I received the following cable from Moshe Sharett, then Prime Minister of Israel:

Urge and beseech you bow to dictates of fate and conscience by accepting presidency federation stop only men of your renowned integrity devotion and personal authority can this juncture avert demoralization upon new constructive chapter for Canadian Zionism stop trust you will not fail us here and your own movement cordial shalom chazakveematz.

It was obvious that I could not say no to this request. I replied:

I could not say no to you stop have accepted presidency at your request stop appreciate your continued faith in me for another term of office stop warm wishes.

Other highlights in the House of Israel were the two Zionist World Congresses to which I led the Canadian delegations. On both occasions I was invited, as President of the ZOC, to sit on the Steering Committee of the Congress, a small committee of approximately thirty people, representative of all of the political parties of Israel and their affiliates throughout the world. There were also delegates from American Hadassah, and representatives of the Women's International Zionist Organization. The Steering Committee is the instrument of the World Congress through which all major recommendations are concluded and eventually brought before the hundreds of delegates that form the World Congress itself. At the Congress the position of the Zionist Organization of Canada was difficult, as the ZOC is basically non-political in its attitudes.

The World Zionist Organization, however, is a political movement. It is mandatory to take a position with one of the political parties at the Congress or face disenfranchisement. Because I wanted to work for the noble and spiritual qualities that are the inspirations for Israel, I always felt uncomfortable being involved in the political. Basic to many of the problems was the use of what is termed the "schlössel" which means "key" in Yiddish. The "key," to oversimplify, meant that those who were appointed to various portfolios, and indeed they were portfolios in many cases, and other significant jobs, would be appointed in relation to their political party influence and representation. Appointments were only one function of the committee meetings. All other matters that concerned the World Organization were brought forward and recommendations prepared.

These steering committee meetings would take, usually, between two and three weeks. We would meet all day and frequently in the evenings too. The meetings were trying, arduous, and frustrating; but in some strange, almost supernatural manner they were productive to a degree that I found astonishing. The meetings were not made easier by my language problem. The Chairman was chosen after having been "decided" before the meeting began. On both occasions, when I was a member of the committee, the Chairman was one of the leading political spokesmen of the MAPAI Party. On both occasions the Chairman began the meeting in Hebrew, only to be interrupted by someone who suggested that although almost everyone in the room could understand Hebrew, there were some exceptions. Someone would then suggest that everyone understood Yiddish and that that should be the language used. This was agreed to unanimously. Regrettably, there was, on both occasions, only one person who could not speak Yiddish–me. Although embarrassed, I had to confess to my inability. The matter was resolved in a most pleasant manner because on both occasions an extremely attractive young woman was assigned to be my interpreter.

At the last Congress I attended, it was made clear to me by my old friend, the late Louis Pincus, Treasurer of the Jewish Agency, that there was a discipline for the countries of the world that he believed should be implemented in Canada. This was that each country should form one Zionist Federation, which would include all Zionist parties. This sounds quite simple. In practice it was most complicated, because each political party worked unilaterally, even though there was collaboration between them in the United Zionist Council, the Chairman of which, by custom, was the President of the ZOC. This council had been formed by my father and I had the pleasure of presiding over it during my years as President. Before I retired after my third term as President of the ZOC, the Zionist Federation, through the strenuous efforts and empathy of many colleagues, was a *fait accompli*.

Soon after I retired as President, the Federation's first convention was held in Toronto, probably the largest Zionist convention ever held in Canada. My friend and colleague, Sam Chait, Q.C., was chosen as its first President.

186

So my presidential years ended, and with this came a new and pleasant beginning. My colleagues throughout the country and particularly in Ottawa would call on me only when they needed me. Little did I think that one such call would cast me in a new role – that of "demonstrator." It became obvious as the years passed that a quiet meeting with a Prime Minister or a Minister of External Affairs might not serve the same purpose as a properly organized demonstration espousing a cause. When Alexei Kosygin visited Ottawa in October 1971, I helped arrange a demonstration of an estimated 10,000 Jewish people to inform the gentleman, in no uncertain terms, that the discrimination against Jewish people in the Soviet must cease and Jews be permitted the essential freedom of leaving the Soviet if they desired. In helping to arrange this vast demonstration, my first call was to my friend Saul Hayes. I told him that we wanted Jewish citizens to come from Montreal, Toronto, and other points and that buses and funds would be needed to accomplish this. In his usual efficient and quiet manner, he and some of his associates made the arrangements. Practically all of the Jewish population of Ottawa was present, and many people arrived on buses from Montreal and Toronto. The demonstration was one of the largest ever held in the capital. It also proved an essential fact that a demonstration, if properly conducted, is, indeed, the most effective instrument for the expression of a just cause.

There were hundreds of placards, many held aloft by young people, that read **Let our people go. Israel needs them and they need Israel.** It is, of course, a sacrilege to all human life to enforce inhuman practices of persecution. Rabbi Gunther Plaut of the Holy Blossom Temple of Toronto, an inmate of a concentration camp in his youth, gave a most impassioned plea.

One incident that I found amusing occurred as these thousands assembled at Strathcona Park, which adjoins the Soviet Embassy. The gentleman in charge of the local police came up to me and said, "Don't worry about a thing. We shall have everything under complete control," which indeed they did. What I found amusing was the fact that we were the demonstrators and the police were going out of their way to protect us against any and all confrontations.

Now, after many active years in the house of Israel, it is gratifying to know that I can still be of use for a majestic cause when necessary. It is also pleasant to feel that, at this point in my life, I am permitted, through the kindness and generosity of many former associates, some ease and relaxation from day-by-day pursuits in Zionist activities in particular and Jewish causes in general.

Chapter IX

And Now...

"And now..." for all intents and purposes began on a fateful day for me, January 1, 1967, the day set aside to mark Canada's Centennial. Audrey and I were invited to join friends on Parliament Hill, where there was to be a gathering of thousands of people, fireworks, and a tremendous birthday cake with 100 candles. The Prime Minister and the Secretary of State, Judy LaMarsh, were to usher in the Centennial year with all the trimmings. Regrettably, we could not make it because that day marked the beginning of my health problems. I awakened at 5:30 on New Year's morning with "shakes" and a temperature of 105°, guilty of the unforgivable medical sin of becoming ill on a weekend in Ottawa. It was almost 2:00 P.M. before Audrey could get a doctor to have me admitted to hospital. This illness was, it turned out, pneumonia and pleurisy.

Finally, out of anxiety and frustration at being unable to find a doctor, Audrey turned to our dear old friend Dr. Shapiro, the host of the Hincks, where I fished with Peter Kriendler. He had been doctor to Mother and Father over all the years and had retired some years before we called upon him again in 1967. He was, of course, not on a hospital staff, and had to call a friend of his, a heart specialist, who did have a hospital affiliation and could get me admitted. "For God's sake!" I told him, "I don't need a heart specialist. I just need a bed in the hospital." After two weeks I insisted on being released, against my doctor's wishes. Three weeks of recuperation followed at home before Audrey and I left for Mexico, to my sister Queene's house, where I was to continue recuperating. Unfortunately, I did not recuperate satisfactorily, and we soon returned to Ottawa.

Soon after we returned, I suffered another serious bout of pneumonia and pleurisy. Over the next year I had to return to hospital frequently–rather like going in and out of a revolving door. These return engagements were marked by seizures that made breathing, which one takes for granted, almost impossible. As a result of these bouts of pneumonia and pleurisy, I was informed that I had developed a chronic, intermittent, obstructive bronchial condition. The seizures must have appeared quite dramatic to my poor wife and family, who often had to rush me off to the emergency ward at the hospital. Audrey was informed by the doctors that there were times when it might have been fatal.

The search for a full diagnosis of the ailment went on for some time. At one point I overheard a doctor say: "I don't really think it is an acquired type of progressive muscular dystrophy, but let's bring in another neurologist and make sure." And so I sat out some weeks of this particular traumatic possibility, eventually to find that muscular dystrophy was one of the things I did not have. The suspect symptoms of the seventeen-pound loss of muscle capacity had probably been caused by certain of the medications. Once all the medical evidence was in, I was informed that I would have to spend the winter months in the sun and that presumably, a sunny but dry climate would be best.

And so we went to Palm Springs, California, where we spent three or four months at the Racquet Club. We had been there before and knew we would enjoy the place, which had been started by Charlie Farrell, the star of silent films. Those of my generation will remember him and Janet Gaynor in *Seventh Heaven*. In the twenties the glamorous gals of the films came to Charlie's place for tennis and the atmosphere of joy he creates. The Racquet Club is now a tennis club with many attractive cottages, two swimming pools, a place where the "beautiful

190

people" of Hollywood continue to gather. Scottie, who was the luncheon *maître d'hôtel* and my good friend, kept my favourite table for me under the awning facing the pool at the club house, the spot where all the "action" was. Besides Eva Gabor, who came every weekend and sat at the next table, there were many people who were fun to see and meet. Audrey was most anxious and disappointed when she did not get to meet Burt Bacharach and Angie Dickinson. When I had not been introduced to Eva Gabor, I finally introduced myself to her and her husband. I told her that I had been to school with Robert Fontaine, the Ottawa author of *The Happy Time*, the Broadway play in which Miss Gabor had her first starring role. Robert and I had been contemporaries at Ottawa's wonderful old high school, the Lisgar Collegiate, a time in Ottawa he immortalized in his play. His father had been the conductor of the orchestra in the local vaudeville house, the Dominion Theatre. Some delightful episodes of French Canadian life in *The Happy Time* concerned the strange guests who, finding themselves "broke" after a week's stay in the Dominion Theatre, would reside at the Fontaine establishment until things picked up. I had seen Miss Gabor in the starring role in New York and thought that she was the most beautiful creature I had ever seen on the stage. She also played it well. When I told her some of these things, she was pleased because she felt that *The Happy Time* was the one really fine play of her career, the one she had enjoyed the most. The world film première of *The Happy Time* was held in Ottawa with Linda Christian as the star and Charles Boyer playing opposite her. The best thing about the film was the party after the *première*. Linda Christian was at our table wearing a provocative *décolleté* gown.

In Palm Springs we saw 21 people, Jerry and Martha, Charlie and Molly Berns. Molly would "hold court," and her court was a great one. She would preside over it wearing hats that were always large and stunning. Although they were usually colossal, Molly's hats were very tailored, made of felt, and in bright colours. They were "only-for-Molly-hats," that only she could wear.

Despite the advantages of the Racquet Club and Palm Springs, the main disadvantage was that it was not the panacea I had hoped for as far as my health was concerned. So, eventually we tried Palm Beach in Florida, which proved to be most beneficial. Ensconced in a pleasant and cheerful flat facing the ocean, with a large swimming pool and gym in the building, we found good friends and a happy and healthy way of life that we still enjoy from November through April every year.

During my enforced long stays away from Ottawa and my business, there were new and disconcerting signs that did not make life pleasant. I was unable to acquire the calibre of senior management that I felt we needed in Freiman's, not only for the present, but for the future development of the business. My son A.J., then about twenty-five, was buyer for all the men's furnishings. Within a year he had nearly doubled the volume of the departments under his control, which for a "youngster" was more than satisfactory to "Dad." My son-in-law, Gordon Roston, was Assistant General Manager. Gordon is a most able administrator and a good merchant, and it had been my hope that, together, he and A.J. would make a great team. At this stage, however, with my being away for such long periods, they needed assistance for the expansion that the company had to continue. They recognized the problem as clearly as I did. In 1969 and 1970 I retired from all of my organizational positions in order to be able to give what precious little time I had left after the winter season to our business. I was deeply flattered when the University of Ottawa named me one of two honorary members of the Board of Trustees and the Zionist Federation made me its Honorary President.

The concerns about our business became increasingly alarming as the months passed. In discussions with professionals in the field, I found that the problems we were experiencing were common to our type of store. Recently, I asked a senior official of a major United States department store trade organization if there was a place for family-oriented department stores of our quality and size in North America. He replied that he did not believe that there are more than twenty-five stores of this kind left in major American cities. With respect to volume, he continued, "Department stores from twenty-five to thirty-five million to over 200 million, such as Hudson's, Neiman Marcus, Bergdorf Goodman, and now even Gimbel's, have found it desirable to merge or sell to larger companies." In his opinion, the reasons are obvious. First, the major family department stores have been unable to attract the superior management necessary to compete with the giant department store chains. This, he believes, was occasioned by the very best people thinking that their chances for promotion were better with the larger corporations than with the smaller ones. Second, he contended that the huge capital requirements needed to continue to expand were often too large for the family-operated business to meet.

In another discussion with one of my old friends, who was the President of one of America's largest department store groups, my friend said: "Unless you are in a market area where you have the opportunity to generate business from seventy-five to 100 million dollars as a minimum, you will not have access to the requirements for professionalism to compete with the large department store chains." He stressed that the companies in his group have ready access to substantial funds and that in practically all cases, they are public companies with more than adequate funds for major capital requirements.

By the summer of 1971, many of these considerations were applicable to our own business. I could not acquire the senior executive talent that A.J., Gordon, and I felt was necessary for future development. Although our financial position was more than satisfactory, the large capital expenditures, which we knew were essential, were a matter of concern. And the Ottawa market was becoming intensely competitive, with no less than eight new department stores under construction or announced.

There was also the family situation. I was most fortunate that even though my sisters had shared the company under my father's will, and I had invited my brothers-in-law to be officials of the company, there had been few times of disagreement, even though, under the will, I was in the position of voting all of the family shares. This brought with it extra responsibility which I felt keenly, not only for my sisters, but also as time went on, for their families.

It was in August of 1971 that the Hudson's Bay Company showed an interest in purchasing our company. There had been proposals before, which had not been interesting to me because it was my desire that my son and son-in-law continue the business. However, in the light of all circumstances, it was decided that I should meet with Mr. Don McGiverin, President of the Hudson's Bay Company. Referring to the proposed new shopping centre in the east end, practically beside our St. Laurent Centre, Mr. McGiverin informed me that the Bay had entered into an arrangement to proceed with the T. Eaton Company and the developers. But should the Bay purchase Freiman's, he would attempt to have his company released from this agreement. We met with the Hudson's Bay Company again and concluded an arrangement in principle in November 1971, with a closing date for sale in December. Part of the arrangement was that our employees would be taken into the Hudson's Bay Company's pension plan. Freiman's had an unofficial and, we believed, a generous pension program. But it was not a funded one. I could not consider leaving my associates, many of whom had worked so closely with me over the many years, without a continuing obligation on the part of the purchaser to look after them.

A.J. and Gordon agreed with me that the risk of continuing with the business was too great. They agreed also that even if they were successful against the tremendous odds, that having to be responsible to my sisters, if they survived me, and eventually to all of their cousins, was not a satisfactory business pursuit. After my death, neither individually nor collectively, under my father's will, could they control the company as I had. It would mean that cousins who would not be running the business could, by right, question, negate or even discontinue my son's or son-in-law's activities with the company. Although this was a fair and responsible business circumstance, it was not one that either my son or son-in-law believed, in the long run, could bring them fulfillment or a happy life. It was the seventies, and they wanted to be "their own people" and "do their own thing." I bless them for this. It is a time not to be bound by grandfathers or fathers but to choose paths which, if followed with vigour and achievement, can lead to their own true freedoms. The choice was obvious to all of us.

It is now nearly six years since the business was sold. There is every indication that the decision was correct. It appears that the voices heard in the quiet spaces of time, the voices of those who "touched" us, gave the right warnings and we did not fall off the rocking horse.

194

Epilogue

I thought that if the book ended in this mood, the reader might assume that the writer had passed to a pleasant and uneventful death. That is not what has happened.

There have been cataclysmic and tragic events – and contrasting moments of unbelievable joy:

—a speech in the crowded Synagogue with 1,400 of the community seated, and countless others standing, when I could scarcely hold back the tears the day after the Munich Massacre.

—a speech from the steps of Parliament to the nation on the Thanksgiving Monday following the Yom Kippur War, demanding our government's sympathy, interest, and effort on behalf of Israel.

—the incredible night at the National Arts Centre when a packed crowd in the Opera House celebrated the twenty-fifth anniversary of the State of Israel, and, along with Ambassador Ted Meron and the Honourable John Turner, I addressed the assembly. Later, in the vast foyer the young were joined by all of us and we danced the Hora* and sang Israeli songs. It seemed but a moment past when I had read, as the President of the Ottawa

*A joyous dance of Israel.

195

Jewish Community Council twenty-five years before, the Declaration of the Independent State of Israel, which had just been proclaimed by David Ben-Gurion in Jerusalem.

—the surge of pride when I heard on the radio that our former employees (now, of course, employees of the Bay), had asked the Ottawa City Council to re-name the street adjoining the store to Freiman Street, a request that the Council approved in January 1974, to perpetuate the name of my father as founder of the store.

These thoughts and others bring warm memories to us as we spend our winters in Palm Beach, Florida, where my doctors feel I should be for six months each year.

Palm Beach is a strange, small island where every hedge, like every poodle, is trimmed perfectly. Not quite as much can be said of its ladies, but God knows, they try. They try on the Monday night theatre openings—black tie, diamonds, photographers, and "the works"—where older ladies with lots of jewels look at even older ladies with even more jewels. Their love of the arts is "so great" that frequently, after seeing it all, many leave after the intermission in their large, chauffeur-driven cars. Or they "try" at the balls that are instruments of a tinsel and unsteady social ladder, shakily built on chairmanships and committees in the hope that their photographs will appear in the local social paper.

But there is Worth Avenue, with all of its "goodies," probably the most beautiful, expensive, and charming small street of shops anywhere. Goodies from Cartier, Van Cleef & Arpels, David Webb, shoes or something from Gucci, who has bought a large hunk of real estate on Worth Avenue to house his expensive "green-red" things. Then there is Martha, who has exquisite things, Saks, and Bonwit's, and countless little shops lining the Rome-like vias that fan out from Worth.

And we swim and walk the beaches directly in front of our apartment and have cocktails and dinner with good friends. Come May, we leave for Ottawa and home, and soon after our return, the flowers bloom, and a totally different life beckons. For a month or so each summer in recent years, we have been invited aboard boats belonging to our dear friends Gertrude and

196

her late husband, Stanley Vineburg,* whose *Don Quixote* is superb; and to Lucy and Irving Cohen of New York, whose *Les Amis* beggars description. We have sailed lazily through the Mediterranean, starting from Cannes and going into most of the small ports along the south of France, and the coast of Italy, and by the yellow-hazed beauty of Sardinia and Corsica. I never wear a tie and shoes, except when ashore. It is a delight to suggest to one's host that we have a noon swim. He then calls the captain and suggests we stop for a bit. The ladder is lowered into the cool, very blue Mediterranean and we have a delicious swim under these ridiculously superb circumstances. Then we have drinks and luncheon on the aft deck. In the evening, we arrive at a small port and have cocktails aboard before wandering around the dock and up a hill to a small, and usually good, restaurant for pasta and the wine of the area.

In the summer of 1976 we met the Cohens at 21 in New York for dinner. Our luggage was taken to Irving's car, waiting beyond the 21 gates. After a splendid dinner, we bid our adieux to Peter K. and headed to the dock. Then, aboard, a farewell drink and we were away. We proceeded first to Nantucket and then Martha's Vineyard, then to Halifax, Charlottetown, and along the Gaspé to the Saguenay to Quebec City and on down to Montreal for the opening of the Olympic Games. After a few days, back to Ottawa to accompany friends to Niagara-on-the-Lake and Stratford, before returning to Montreal for the spectacular closing of the Games.

So it goes along pleasantly, if somewhat languidly decadent, and I console myself with the thought that this is literally what "the doctor ordered."

And despite some of the social idiocies of a winter in Palm Beach, one thing cannot be changed—the beauty of that little island, with the Atlantic on one side and Lake Worth on the other. On a beautiful day—and most days are beautiful—the water is very blue, and the ocean breaks with whipcream blobs on top as it rolls to the shore. It would also be unfair not to note the beauty of the ocean-front estates and their hedges and

*A Montreal industrialist who died in December of 1975.

197

gardens–and the refreshing cleanliness of the entire town. Despite my feelings about the so-called "social" scene, we return each year because we like Palm Beach, and one must see the community in its real perspective. It is like engaging and amusing theatre in which many people try to star–and so few make it. Also, our days are pleasant–spent on the sun-drenched beaches and at pools with good friends, none of whom "try" for parts in the Palm Beach scenario.

Then there is the return to Ottawa.

And as I walk by the Hudson's Bay Company on Freiman Street, I think with nostalgia of the many years past when I walked down this same street with my grandfather and with my mother and father. Today, I walk there with my family. As we walk, we look back on the good things that have happened and forward with confidence to the good things to come.

We have happiness in our son A.J.–and his beautiful, intelligent sabra* bride, Ruth, and are confident in the success of his new undertaking, A.J. Freiman Enterprises, Ltd. In addition, we take joy in their acquisition of the Robertson Galleries. It is prideful to us also that our son-in-law, Gordon, advanced to senior management in the Hudson's Bay Company as General Manager of their stores in the Ottawa region. Gordon, however, wanted to pursue other activities. Therefore, after his stint with the Bay he left to become an adviser to the Anti-Inflation Board, and is presently adviser to the Department of the Secretary of State.

It is no doubt a natural thing for a father to have a special feeling for a daughter. I have this feeling for Margo, still, as I see her now, an attractive young woman who provides her children with love, direction, and strength, just as Audrey did in our home.

There is leisure time now for us to walk around the corner to Margo and Gordon's house and play with their children by the pool. It is a time not only to reflect, but to encourage one's children without feeling the impatience that a pressured life can create.

Audrey never wanted to "run," and it is sheer joy for her to

*Native-born Israeli.

198

see her husband finally "walking." Today we will drive up the parkway through Gatineau Park, marvelling still at the richness of foliage and scenery. We shall have lunch at the small tea room there, and then a walk in the woods. Together, tonight, we shall hear good music in the Arts Centre. It is a time for us, our children, and theirs, to plan for tomorrow—a time to look forward together.

September 1977